Persuasion Dark Psychology Secrets

The Art of Persuasion is not Evil,

it's Just a Tool

The Deep Study in the Dark side of Psychology

to Master Mental Manipulation

and Body Language

Table of Contents

- INTRODUCTION 6
- PART 1 13
- CHAPTER 1: WHAT IS PERSUASION? 13
  - UNDERSTANDING PERSUASION AND ITS SIGNIFICANCE 14
  - CHANGING MINDSETS 15
  - DISPUTE MANAGEMENT 16
  - GREATER SALES 17
  - CAREER ADVANCEMENT 18
- CHAPTER 2: HOW TO BECOME PERSUASIVE? 20
  - FACTORS AFFECTING THE POWER AND EFFECT OF PERSUASION, ACCORDING TO ROBERT CIALDINI 21
- CHAPTER 3: WHY IS PERSUASION IMPORTANT? 27
  - WHY DO YOU NEED PERSUASION? 27
  - PERSUASION AND YOUR DAILY LIFE 30
- CHAPTER 4: HISTORY OF PERSUASION 35
  - MODERN-DAY ARISTOTLE 37
- CHAPTER 5: MODELS OF PERSUASION 40
  - PERSUASION AND MANIPULATION: KNOW THE DIFFERENCE 43
  - PERSUASIVE TECHNIQUES TO KNOW AND USE 45
- CHAPTER 6: MANIPULATION IS NOT EVIL; IT'S JUST A TOOL 48
  - WHAT IS MANIPULATION? 48
  - THE QUALITIES OF A MANIPULATIVE PERSON 52
- CHAPTER 7: MASTER YOUR EMOTION IS THE KEY 55
  - WHAT IS EMOTIONAL INFLUENCE? 55
  - PRINCIPLES OF EMOTIONAL INFLUENCE 57
  - HOW TO RECOGNIZE AND OVERCOME NEGATIVE EMOTIONS THAT CONTROL YOUR LIFE 62
    - RECOGNIZING NEGATIVE EMOTIONS 63
    - OVERCOMING NEGATIVE EMOTIONS 69
    - BECOME AWARE 72
    - PRACTICE MINDFULNESS DAILY 73
    - DISTINGUISHING HELPFUL FROM UNHELPFUL THOUGHTS 74
- CHAPTER 8: KEY ELEMENTS OF PERSUASION 77
- CHAPTER 9: PERSUASION SKILLS 81

PERSUASIVE LANGUAGE 81
SIX THEORIES OF PSYCHOLOGICAL MANIPULATION 82
CHAPTER 10: HOW TO INFLUENCE PEOPLE? 90
BRAINWASHING 90
HYPNOSIS 91
MANIPULATION 92
PERSUASION 92
DECEPTION 93
CHAPTER 11: METHODS OF PERSUASION 95
WIN-WIN CONCEPT 95
BUILD YOUR TRUST 96
INTENSITY 96
TO SELECT 96
MYSTERY 97
SHORTAGE 97
PERCEIVED VALUE 97
BE A GOOD PERSON 97
MAKE IT CLEAR WHAT THEY'RE MISSING 98
BE AN OBSERVER 98
HONESTY AND RELIABILITY 98
GET OVER YOUR IDEA 99
OVERSIMPLIFY YOUR IDEA 99
PUT YOURSELF IN A NEUTRAL POSITION 99
CHANGE THE ENVIRONMENT TO YOUR ADVANTAGE 100
SPEAK QUICKLY 100
CREATING NEEDS 101
TOUCHING SOCIAL NEEDS 101
USE OF MEANINGFUL AND POSITIVE WORDS 101
USE OF FOOT TECHNIQUE 102
USE OF ORIENTATION FROM BIG TO SMALL 102
USE OF RECIPROCITY 102
LIMITATION TECHNIQUE 103
CHAPTER 12: PRINCIPLES OF PERSUASION 104
THE CONCEPTS THAT MAKE IT WORK 108
CHAPTER 13: THE ULTIMATE GUIDE TO ENHANCE YOUR PERSUASION TECHNIQUES 111
EMPATHY-BASED PERSUASIVE TECHNIQUES 111
MIRROR BASED PERSUASIVE TECHNIQUES 112
OTHER PERSUASIVE TECHNIQUES 113

BE PERSUASIVE BY CONNECTING EMOTIONALLY, NOT RATIONALLY 114
- THE MORAL BEHIND PERSUASION TECHNIQUES 115
- THE INTENSITY OF CONSCIOUS PERSUASION 116

PART 2 .... **119**

CHAPTER 14: WHAT IS DARK PSYCHOLOGY? 119
- HOW DARK PSYCHOLOGY WORKS? 122
- UNDERSTANDING DARK PERSUASION 127
- UNMASKING THE DARK PERSUADER 128

CHAPTER 15: INDOCTRINATION STRATEGIES 130
- HOW CAN YOU INFLUENCE OTHERS? 134

CHAPTER 16: BRAINWASHING 139
- THE CONSCIOUS LEVEL 141
- THE UNCONSCIOUS OR BEHAVIORAL PSYCHOLOGY 142
- BIOLOGICAL PSYCHOLOGY 144

CHAPTER 17: BODY LANGUAGE 146
- UNDERSTANDING WHAT MY BEHAVIOR DISPLAY 147
- HOW CAN ANYONE READ PEOPLE? 156
- HOW TO DETECT ROMANTIC INTEREST IN A MOMENT 165
- HOW TO SPOT AN INSECURE PERSON 169
- HOW TO SPOT THE LIARS 170

CHAPTER 18: HYPNOTIC INDUCTION 175
- WHAT ARE THE DIFFERENCES BETWEEN HYPNOSIS ON STAGE AND IN REAL LIFE? 178
- WHAT ARE THE ADVANTAGES OF HYPNOTIZING SOMEONE? 181

CHAPTER 19: TECHNIQUES OF DARK PSYCHOLOGY 184
- THE DOOR IN THE FACE! 185
- FOOT IN THE DOOR 186
- "YES-SET" TECHNIQUE 187
- LINGUISTIC PRESUPPOSITION 188
- REVERSE PSYCHOLOGY 189
- NEGATIVE HIDDEN COMMANDS 191

CHAPTER 20: UNDERSTANDING DECEPTION 193
- DARK OR NOT? 193
- THE DECEPTION SPECTRUM 195
- SIGNS OF DECEPTION 197
- TIPS USED IN SPOTTING A LIAR 200

CHAPTER 21: SPEED-READING PEOPLE 204

- PAY ATTENTION TO CONTEXT 211
- STAY OBJECTIVE 212
- EXAGGERATED TRAITS 213
- LOOK FOR INCONSISTENCY 214
- **CONCLUSION** **216**

Introduction

The idea behind being a persuasive person, which is the main objective of persuasion, is to get something in return. There is no sense in practicing the art of persuasion if there is nothing desired in return. Persuasion means to cause someone to do something specific. Therefore, some sort of gain is desired, some sort of result.

To know the intended result of the persuasive effort, there must be a defined desired outcome. The person doing the persuading wants something tangible, something definable. But what do they want? That is completely up to them to decide, which often happens before they engage in any form of persuasion, which is exactly what they hope to achieve at the end of the conversation.

This is what is meant by defining desired outcomes. The desired thing must be decided before any kind of persuasive tactics begin so that the person doing the persuading understands the desired outcome.

For instance, a particular office staff decides to hold a meeting to decide the new office location because the old office seems small and cramped, and business is growing and thus needs more room to continue its growth. So an office meeting will take place where the new location will be decided upon. This is the first step in defining the desired outcome, knowing what the proposed outcome is. In this case, it is the location of the new office.

So the meeting has been set for a particular time and place. Finished, right? Wrong! Without some order and organization, the meeting will be unproductive, and the desired outcome probably will not happen. The meeting is crucial to the desired outcome. Without a specific plan, the meeting is nothing more than people in an office meeting in one room to make conversation.

So now it is necessary to set up the meeting; to have a plan as to how the meeting will proceed. Since this is a meeting that comprises the entire office staff, there might not be any need to decide who to invite since everyone would be in attendance. So, the after step would be to create the meeting agenda; Will there be time for questions? Will certain people be invited to participate by offering specific recommendations for the new location? How will the ultimate decision be reached? All these factors need to be decided before the meeting begins.

When beginning the meeting, be sure to mention the desired outcome. Let everyone know exactly what they are there to discuss. Make sure everyone involved knows and understands the desired outcome. Set a specific time for discussion and a time when the decision will be made. When the meeting reaches the end of its prescribed time, restate the objective and determine if a decision can be made or if more research is needed.

An outcome is nothing more than a result that can be seen and measured. It is the consequence of the action. It is the conclusion that comes from persuading someone to do something. Four things will need to be decided in any desired outcome before the desired outcome can be decided. Those four things are; is the desire for something specific there? Is something already owned needing to be kept? Who should be connected with, and how? What skills are required to achieve the desired outcome?

It is important to decide these things because the underlying objectives will affect how the outcome will be gained. It is similar to a football game where there is a defensive team and an offensive team. One group attacks the opposing team, and one group defends against the attacks from the opposing teams. Each team will have a different set of priorities and procedures. Their desired outcomes will be quite different from one another. Each team will need to decide what it is they want to learn, defend, or acquire. The goal will determine the game plan.

Some sort of change needed has been identified and will be achieved. The path to achievement begins with setting a goal. The end of this journey is the desired outcome. It is necessary to understand that these are two separate entities that work together to achieve a result.

A goal is a destination. An outcome is a specific thing; it can be seen and measured. While setting the goal is vital to receiving the outcome, they are very different and should be treated.

Goals always have reasons behind them. Something that is thought of as being necessary to happiness, wealth, health, or just because it is truly desired is just not there. Whatever the reason is, it is that exact reason that drives forward progress toward the desired outcome. To progress, to go forward to the goal, that goal and the idea of achieving it must be firmly entrenched in your mind. Without a steady focus on the goal, there is no possibility that the goal will ever be reached.

Imagine going to work every day for fifteen years, doing the same job every day. Imagine this is a job that needed college courses, so it was a chosen job. During the past fifteen years, doing the same job every day has been rewarding and profitable. There have been several promotions, the last of which came with a private secretary and a lovely large office. Several other people, who have not been working here quite as long, are now the team that directly reports to you every Monday in this large new office.

But all of a sudden, going to work becomes somewhat boring. The job just does not bring the amount of satisfaction it once did. The problem is not in the job itself but the person who is doing the job. What seemed so right all those years now feels so wrong. What has desired her is more interaction with people. A new skill has to emerge in managing other people: taking raw recruits and molding them into productive team members with a bright future. That is the job that brings happiness and satisfaction.

But while this thought has been firmly entrenched in mind for months now, no changes have been made to get closer to the goal of that type of occupation, and so every Monday morning is filled with team meetings, every day is filled with spreadsheets, and every Friday is filled with boundless joy that another work week has passed. Why?

The answer to that is procrastination. Whether intentional or unintentional, procrastination has ruined many good intentions. Unintentional procrastination does happen sometimes. Everyone has that moment of "oops! I meant to take care of that today. I'll get to it first thing in the morning." That is unintentional; something was forgotten. Intentional procrastination means knowing something needs to be done but putting it off until whenever. Many people do this with dreams and desires, especially those that will require extra work to accomplish or simply just a big leap of faith. Changing careers when one is firmly established is a scary thing. But what someone wants at twenty is not necessarily what they'd want at forty. People change. Their hearts change. They must be willing to follow their dreams and make them a reality. But people procrastinate out of fear.

So ask these three questions:

- What exactly am I afraid of? Do I fear losing a great job that will pay for my kid's college because I may not be able to find one that pays as well? What if I have to take a pay cut and can no longer pay the mortgage? What happens if I lose my health insurance? These are all valid questions that must be addressed when considering a large change in employment.

- What will I gain if I can conquer this fear? What will great gain be realized? Will it be a new job, a new career that is more in line with current life goals? Maybe the real dream is the chance to help other people.

- What do I do to fight this fear? Accept the fear as real. Acknowledge its existence. Then make a plan to reach the new goal and proceed without waiting. Go forward without procrastination.

Now, it is time to set a goal to make this dream a reality. Identify the goal as specifically. The more specific the goal, the better the chance is to realize that goal. Vague goals are nothing more than wishes. It is as simple as the difference between "I want to lose weight" and "I want to lose twenty pounds." The second statement is a specific goal that can be measured as work towards it progresses.

Know exactly what is desired as a reward when the goal is achieved. If the goal is weight loss, perhaps the reward is wearing that dress featured in the store window. If the goal is learning how to swim, then maybe the goal is to swim in the ocean for the first time. Plan how this goal will be achieved. Think about the senses used along the way and how they will make this progress easier or more difficult.

Visualize the plan and try to imagine any possible obstacles. That does not mean putting the obstacles in the path, but in being aware of the possibility that they might crop up and having a plan to defeat them. If the intended goal involves weight loss, what will be the plan for coping with the buffet during the holiday season? If the goal is to complete classes online, what happens if the internet goes out or the computer crashes? It is necessary to have a back-up plan to deal with life's little emergencies.

What will be used for markers along the way to track progress toward the goal? If the goal is weight loss, then perhaps a wall chart with every five pounds lost marked in red. Perhaps a thermometer drawing, with the mercury bulb's goal at the top, and the thermometer is filled in gradually with every pound lost. Have a system in place to track these milestones.

Be aware that working toward any goal might come with negatives attached. Changing careers will most certainly mean a change in income. What if the career change means moving to another state? Is that a viable option? An extreme amount of weight loss will mean constantly refreshing the wardrobe. It is important to be aware of anything that might be seen as a negative effect of reaching the goal. These must be acceptable, or the goal will need to be changed.

And when little distractions occur along the way, do not let them cancel out any progress that has already been made. Life happens. All roads have bumps in them. Even Shakespeare knew that no matter how good the plan was, it might not work. So acknowledge that little bumps in the road will happen and have a plan to overcome them.

PART 1

Chapter 1: What Is Persuasion?

Persuasion is something that we experience daily. We are going to be persuaded by friends and family to help out on occasion. We will see many advertisements from companies that want to persuade us to purchase their products and not from competitors. We see persuasion so often that it is sometimes hard to realize that it could be bad and that a manipulator could try to use this against us.

How does one get people to think and behave differently and to follow their path? There will be many subtle ways to press your agenda without turning everyone off and making it seem like you have some sinister plan in the making. When it comes to persuasion, Robert Cialdini is well respected for some of his ideas on persuasion and how to do it successfully, whether your intentions are good or not.

According to Cialdini, six principles can be used to help out with the ideas of persuasion, and these six principles are going to include:

- Reciprocity: This is where you will do a small favor for someone, and then right away ask them to do one back.

- Commitment and consistency: This one holds the target of doing something because they have done it in the past.

- Social proof: This is when you convince the target to do something because it is popular, and everyone is doing it.

- Authority: Your target is more likely to do something if they believe you are an authority on that topic.

- Likeability: If you can become likable and see you as a friend, they are more likely to do what you ask.

- Scarcity: This is the fear that an item will be in short supply, so they want to get it.

Understanding Persuasion And Its Significance

The main aim of every negotiation is to agree on an issue. In coming to that agreement, a major skill you need is persuasion. You should be able to persuade and convince the other party to agree with you.

Being good at persuasion is a vital part of a successful negotiation. It is a very important skill that you and everyone intend to have fruitful negotiations or intend to influence others. Persuasion is effectively marketing and selling your point of view to the other party. You have to persuade the other party to understand your viewpoint and even to accept it.

As an entrepreneur or an individual going into a negotiation, you should convince others to accept your ideas or your stance. For example, it is persuasion that would help you get your employer to increase your salary when you are negotiating a salary raise, and this would only happen if you can convince your employer about how valuable you have been and how a salary raise for you would be beneficial to both you and the company.

Persuasion is mostly giving people reasons why they should do something to be convinced to do it.

Contrary to what people believe about persuasion being a talent, it is a skill that can be learned and can be honed through practice. If you are still in doubt about why persuasion is important in negotiation and why you need to learn how to persuade people, here are some reasons.

Changing Mindsets

This appears to be the most apparent benefit of persuasion; however, it needs to be reiterated because of its importance.

When people come to the negotiation table, they come with their beliefs, mindsets, and attitudes. Sometimes, these beliefs or mindsets do not favor you, which means you have to change them through persuasion.

The mindsets or beliefs do not even have to be about the negotiation or the issue at hand. Sometimes they are about you, and you can use persuasion to change how the other party views you.

For example, a former negotiation with an earlier client earned you a bad reputation in the industry, the status of a wise businessperson who everyone should be wary of when transacting business. Now, when people have to do business with you, they are so careful, and they are always on the defense so much that the negotiation process rarely goes smoothly. With persuasion, you can convince the client that the reputation is false. You can influence them to stop being on the defense, and you will have a smooth negotiation process and get the best possible outcome.

Dispute Management

Paul is in a negotiation between the IT company he works at and a prospective client. A tactless colleague at the meeting has just said something the prospective client finds annoying. Tempers are flaring; words are being exchanged.

Paul decides to step in and do something. He is known as a tension diffuser at the office who can influence people to do his bidding. He calmly speaks to the client and then to his colleague. Apologies are exchanged, and everyone goes back to doing what they were doing earlier.

When you can persuade people as a skill, you will be able to deal with any disputes while negotiating. Sometimes, deals do not go through because they are open or latent disputes or rising tensions, and the two parties have gotten to a point where their emotions cloud their judgment. It takes persuasion skill to handle this and ensure that everyone goes back to the negotiation table and makes the deal.

This benefit of persuasion is particularly important because you should build relationships that leave room for further negotiation and business transactions after the initial negotiation.

Greater Sales

Stella is a businesswoman looking to sell her products. However, she is experiencing a drought when it comes to getting customers to buy the products she is selling. Also, there is the problem of competitors who have established brands in the industry getting most of the patronage. Stella wants customers to patronize her business. She wants customers to buy her products. Not only is Stella looking for new customers who have not purchased a similar product, but she is also hoping to get some of her competitors' customers. She needs to convince these customers to buy her products.

When you are promoting your product or service to a customer, your ability to persuade them to see why they should patronize is vital to making any successful sale. You need to convince your target market that you understand their needs and know how to provide great solutions to those needs.

Persuasion during sales will help you show the customer the merits of giving you their money. Persuasion is important for negotiating even the customer's price; if you want to make a sales deal happen, learn how to be persuasive.

Career Advancement

Everyone wants to grow. Whether it is transitioning to a new job or getting a promotion and a corresponding pay raise, career advancement is always welcome.

Career advancement also involves some negotiation. From negotiating your salary to negotiating with the firm's management you work for a promotion and a pay raise; you need to have good negotiation skills to get your desired outcome.

When it comes to getting your desired outcome in advancing your career, persuasion plays a significant role. Suppose you are applying for a new job. In that case, you should persuade your prospective employer to increase the initial offer that was made and pay you either the amount you are asking for or something close to that which would still be favorable to you. If you already work at a firm and you would like to take on more responsibility, you would like to be promoted, or you want a pay raise, you need to convince the firm's management to get the desired outcome.

One good thing about persuasion is that its effects are not limited to a single person. You can use it for large audiences. Suppose you are trying to pitch a product or service to a room full of potential investors beyond persuading one person to invest in the product. In that case, you can persuade all the potential investors to make your great offers.

After discovering how persuasion can be beneficial to you, you should learn the types of persuasion. Learning the types of persuasion is a step in the right direction for learning how to wield persuasion as a valuable skill while negotiating.

Chapter 2: How to Become Persuasive?

How is it that some people are so good at convincing others to do things? How do some people manage to persuade others into things they wouldn't normally do? The skills of a manipulator and situation a person determines the extent to which one can be influenced. How much can a person persuade you is determined by your current state? For instance, if you are lonely, hungry, tired, or even needy somehow, then the chances of you being persuaded rise. Simply put, you can get a hungry man to do anything so long as you promise him a plate of food.

So, ensuring that all your basic needs are met, emotionally and physically, can make you less susceptible to con artists who appear to offer solutions to them but as for too much in exchange. Something that seems to meet a certain need in your life, more so basic, can seem very persuasive. One might think that he/she will notice when a person is trying to manipulate him or her but, the techniques used to persuade are very subtle, and some of the tools used are very basic; thus, we are not always conscious of them.

According to psychologist Robert Cialdini, there are six major persuasion principles, and they are not always used for bad intentions. He explains that if a person used these skills to improve others' lives, it is a good thing. If someone persuaded the other not to drink and drive, then that is a good thing.

Factors Affecting the Power And Effect Of Persuasion, According To Robert Cialdini

Reciprocity

The first and most common principle affecting persuasion is reciprocity. You will find that you feel obligated to do something in return to show appreciation whenever a person does you a favor. Interestingly, this feeling is in the subconscious mind such that we are not aware of its presence. A statement such as "I owe you one" or "I am much obliged" is used to show someone that we are grateful for their assistance and hope and help them whenever needed because of something they have done for us.

A manipulator who knows these techniques can use a small favor to get you to reciprocate. Sometimes, this manipulator will look for something that you need and step in to help. In return, they will ask for something that is way out of your bracket. And because 'you are obliged,' you will reciprocate the favor. The concept of reciprocity has been used widely by companies. First, they offer free samples to customers who will then feel the need to give back by buying the item even if it does not meet the standards.

One of my friends does not accept free samples in malls, so I asked her why she does not sample the designer perfumes offered. She said, "That is how we get trapped. You sample it, and the salesperson talks you into buying it even though it is overpriced. And since you already sampled, reciprocity comes into play." That explanation made a lot of sense to me.

Of course, some people do favors for others without expecting anything in return, but you have to beware. Others are manipulative, and in the majority of us, the feeling of owing someone is a very big decision influencer.

Self-Consistency

Another principle of persuasion is self-consistency. Robert Cialdini found some people are more likely to stick with an idea or goal they committed to (verbally or in writing) because of self-image. Some people associate commitment with self-image and personality. Though there is nothing wrong with being committed, to some extent is not justified. These people who apply the principle of self-consistency can get so lost in their idea that even when it becomes invalid, they continue to honor it.

We like to present a consistent image to the world and ourselves. As such, it becomes hard to leave a thing we started even after realizing that it is not worthy. Gradually, we develop a sense of sympathy for the idea we have been following, such that quitting is hard.

The term brainwashing is derived from a Chinese expression that means 'to wash the brain.' The concept of brainwashing became clear during the Korean War. The Chinese who were instructed to repeat certain pro-Communist and anti-American ideas to prisoners gradually began to believe their statements. A belief you practiced but did not believe gradually becomes part of you.

People who follow the lead bully often start out doing small favors and tasks. After a while, it becomes hard to leave the practice because of maintaining face in public. So, when the lead bully becomes selfish to others, the followers cannot make a different choice. Do not underestimate the power of the fear of loneliness. Do not undermine the need to be consistent and to feel. It can make a person do things he/she would not do under normal circumstances.

Social Proof

The power of social proof is something no one can deny. We are mostly herd creatures of society in many ways. As human beings, we tend to follow what others are doing. If a million people are doing a certain thing, then they cannot be wrong, so we follow them. Do you think people would wear pants that revealed their underwear if no one else was doing it? If a large number of people start to sing along some weird songs, chances are, others will join the crowd. We tend to do things done by other people.

Of course, we have to realize that there are things done by crowds with perfectly good reasons. However, there is a 'madness of the crowd' concept whereby we do not want to think for ourselves. That is a very strong persuasion tool used by manipulators and persuaders.

Perceived Authority

One powerful persuader is a confident, authoritative attitude. Have you ever walked into an office with nothing but confidence and authority and gotten what you want? Do you understand why they say confidence is very important during an interview? An authoritative manner can persuade people. Anyone will think that you have power and knowledge just because of a confident appearance.

Most of the ex-Nazis explained that they just followed the orders of their leaders. Just because someone with authority said it, then it must be correct. Titles, too, add to the perceived authority. For example, a teacher, a scientist, or a king can say anything, and it appears correct.

In the 1960s, Stanley Milgrams did experiments revealing that most people can carry out highly questionable and cruel acts so long as the person asking has the perceived authority. The problem with this [principle of perceived authority is that it can easily be faked by putting on the appropriate uniform, speaking in a certain manner, and behaving in a particular way. All of us are capable of falling for fake authority. Once again, we allow someone to think for us.

Likeability

On the face, there is nothing particularly sinister about likability. Interestingly, it has been identified as the fifth principle of persuasion. Likable people are very persuasive. Everyone can easily fall for the charm of a likable person. It has been found that people are more likely to purchase things from someone they like, and that is why many companies look for likable salespersons. Likable people are often attractive, and if they try too hard, it comes across as smarmy. However, if we truly like them, there are high chances of us purchasing things from them. In fact, how many times have you heard a person who was conned say, "but he/she seemed nice"?

The world has confirmed that attractive people are more likable, cleverer, braver, and better than plain ones. That mentality is termed as 'the Halo effect.' The challenge is, even the most attractive people might not have pure intentions towards you.

Scarcity

The fact that gold is rare makes it more interesting to find and purchase. You have heard people say that if diamonds grew on trees, no one would care about them, but now that they are rare, we value them. What makes them so precious is their scarcity – there are not many of them around. That is why offers in the malls have deadlines. It is also the reason why you hear salespeople saying, "We can only give this offer till Monday" or "This offer is valid while this stock lasts, and people are buying a lot." The thought that these items will soon be scarce will make you want to make a purchase. The perceived scarcity adds value to the product.

In the case of people, these scarcity experiences run deep and affect us more than we think. For instance, if we have a partner or spouse who is grumpy, moody, and disagreeable most of the time, we might fall into the trap of feeling extremely grateful when they display a shred of happiness. In such a case, we will be manipulated into doing things to get a glimpse of that rare happy moment. Their pleasant behavior is scarce and is, therefore, very valuable to us.

Psychologist B.F Skinner, a behaviorist, found that inconsistent rewards are more compulsive and addictive because of the scarcity. Therefore, a dog that is not always rewarded with food will act more compulsively than food used to food now and then. Unbelievable but true, if gambling involved sure wins all the time, it would not be as interesting. Maybe the person who keeps going back to the abusive relationship is just addicted to the few good times in that relationship. So, be on the safe side and stay aware of the people using the scarcity principle on you.

Beware of the people using these principles. Do not get persuaded by manipulators just because you are under the influence of scarcity or liking. Do not fall for fake authority or social proof tricks. It is okay to change if you find that something is not working as expected. If need be, lose the self-consistency and need to reciprocate.

Chapter 3: Why Is Persuasion Important?

Why Do You Need Persuasion?

We all like to think that we are people with minds of our own. The idea of someone being able to wield power over our ability to analyze and decide for ourselves can be frightening. However, it is a basic fact of life that every decision we make is based on several different influences on our lives. We make all of our decisions based on both internal and external pressures for us to do so. We may have made up our minds in one direction, and then something happens, and we start thinking in an entirely different way. The reality is that changing our minds is a natural part of the human psyche and mastering this skill is just part of being human.

Unlike any other creation that walks this earth, humans are some of the most social of all living species. Our ability to communicate is key to our survival and is the main reason why we go to such great lengths to make sure that others understand us. We even exercise our communication skills without even thinking about them. Think about the automatic mental game your mind plays as soon as you enter a room. Immediately the brain scans the room searching for those people that we view as important to us. We look for our friends, for those who think and act as we do, and those we would hope we can build a connection to. Our minds do this instinctively; there is no planning or plotting involved, but the result is that we surround ourselves with people we'd like to influence us or those we feel confident we can influence.

Our brains divide our social connections into two camps. The first group includes those we perceive will benefit us in the future, and the second are those with whom we connect emotionally or have some common bond or goals we share.

There are many aspects in our life that require us to be persuasive:

Marketing

If you are in any business type, your ability to attract and keep customers will be directly affected by how persuasive you can be. Any business can get off to a good start with supportive friends and family members, but to give your business any kind of staying power, you'll have to convince strangers to trust in you and the products or services you offer.

Management

Another crucial aspect of your business is managing employees and getting them to follow your directions. Part of being a good manager is being able to influence another person's behavior. But the skill is not limited to business; rather, it can also be used when interacting with family members, in social circles, and a wide range of other areas of one's life. Anytime you need to motivate someone to follow your directions, you'll need persuasive speaking skills.

Teaching

A large part of teaching is influencing your students in some way or another. Whether you're teaching pre-school or at the university level, getting students to grasp your lessons and apply them to their lives will require you to have some pretty good persuasive arguments. A good teacher knows how to guide people's behavior, so you need to know how people respond to others and use that to your advantage.

Charities

Charities use persuasive speech in every aspect of their business. Their goals are to motivate people to volunteer, make donations, and to speak out against and for all sorts of causes, often without any form of compensation. A charity's success will depend largely on how effective they are in connecting with their audience emotionally and moving them to action. To do this, you need to influence people's opinions.

For Help

Whether you need someone to bag your groceries at the supermarket or you want that landlord to choose you over a hundred other tenants, it is the power of influence that will move them to do so. It is one thing to ask someone to do something for you and another entirely to persuade them to do it. Knowing how to request so people are more likely to respond can get you the help you need.

Opinions

Whether you're an environmentalist, politician, or social activist, persuasion can make you more successful.

Because persuasion is a natural part of our mental and emotional fabric, it is a key element in giving our life foundation. Everyone uses it, so whether you become a persuasion expert or not, the reality is simple. If you're not doing the persuading, the odds are quite high that you're being persuaded yourself.

Persuasion and Your Daily Life

Persuasion is unbelievable and of utmost importance in our world today.

Almost every human interaction involves an attempt to persuade or influence others to the speaker's way of thinking.

This is true regardless of professions, age, sex, philosophical beliefs, or religion.

People are always trying to convince each other.

It is undeniable that all human beings want to have the ability to persuade others, so they will hear, believe, and support them.

The people who can effectively use persuasion tactics will always find excellent employment opportunities even if the economy is experiencing problems.

If you can persuade other people, then you have a power that you can use to make your life better.

Think about every person who has influenced you to do your best and become successful in your entire life.

Persuasive people can improve lives, avoid wars, and keep adolescents free from drugs or alcohol.

However, some persuasive people can also destroy lives, start wars, and convince kids to try drugs or alcohol.

That means persuasion is a powerful ability you can use for positive or negative things, depending on your motives.

On the other hand, it would be best to use this power to increase self-improvement and overall growth for the entire community.

There are many reasons why you would want to use persuasion. It usually has something to do with convincing other people to do something that you would like. Most of us have heard about persuasion, and we associate it with things that are not always the best. For example, we may be used to seeing persuasion being used as a manipulation technique, which is only brought out when we want to force someone to act in a certain way. Or we may think of persuasion as the annoying techniques used in advertising, ones that we hear all the time and are probably really sick of.

But these are just a few examples of persuasion, and in fact, they are a little bit misleading. Persuasion is not manipulation, and, for the communication to be considered persuasion, the other party needs to have free will. You can use certain language to try and convince them that one method is better than another one, or you can try to use a little peer pressure to convince them that they should act in a specific way, but the fact remains that the other person you are talking to should have the free will to choose.

Plus, there are many good examples of how you can use persuasion to your advantage and the other person's advantage. If you go out one night to a new restaurant and love the food, it is still a form of persuasion if you try to convince the other person to visit that restaurant. If you want to see a specific movie, listing off the reasons they should come along with you can be persuasive.

There are no rules that state that the other person has to give up something or be harmed for this to be persuasion. Yes, advertising is persuasion, and it does ask the other person to give up their money and even some time to go and get the item, but not all persuasion works this way. Any time you try to convince the person to act a specific way or try to help influence their decisions, regardless of how the outcome affects you, can be considered persuasion.

Persuasion is all around us, and while we may think that we are smart enough to recognize it all of the time and make our own decisions, this is not always the case. Yes, most types of advertising are not all that convincing unless you were actively looking for a specific product and are comparing your options, but there are many times when persuasion will come into our lives, and we don't even realize that we are being persuaded to act in a certain way.

For example, if a friend tells you that there is a new place to go and have dinner some time and then asks you to come along a few weeks following, how would you respond? It is most likely unless you had made other plans ahead of time, that you would agree to go with them. You had the free will, but because this person is your friend and you value their opinion, you would likely go to the restaurant with them.

As you can see, there are many different ways that persuasion can be present in your daily life. You will find persuasion all around the place, and when you learn how to use it for yourself, rather than always letting someone else do it to you, it can make a change in how your life is going. It will help you influence your friends and family, and it will help you get the things you want out of life.

There are a lot of times when you would want to bring persuasion into your life. Some of the reasons to use persuasion include:

- To sell products: one of the most prominent places where you will see a lot of persuasions is product sales. Businesses spend billions of dollars each year trying to persuade consumers that they need them better than any other. And while some advertisements are obvious and easy to ignore, many of them are pretty advanced, and you may fall victim to persuasion if you are not careful.

- To get help with something: if you need someone to take some time out of their day to help you out, you will need to use persuasion to get them to do this. Some people will be willing to help out with it simply because you are their friend, and they like you, but sometimes you need to use some phrases and techniques to get the results.

- To convince someone to try something: any time you would like someone to try something new, whether it is a new restaurant, a show, or something else, you are using persuasion. It is often meant to be helpful; you want the other person to enjoy themselves, and you think they will like the new place.

Chapter 4: History of Persuasion

The persuasion can be traced back to Greek origins. It was used as a tool by great orators to get their message across to the common folk. For a country that has created the political frameworks behind democracy, persuasion was immensely popular. If you have ever taken an advanced writing class that went over rhetorical analysis, you might recognize the three rhetorical modes of pathos, ethos, and logos. Aristotle billed these as the three main appeals that an orator could make to move their audience.

Its usage implies that the audience is a malleable entity, like putty. A skilled orator's words can manipulate the audience like a child might manipulate a piece of putty. Other times, persuasion is used to rile up an already popular cause, to begin with, but that had been up to that point undisclosed.

The three rhetorical modes are important because they represent three different attack vectors that a manipulator might use to persuade their audience. Again, any form of persuasion is a type of mental manipulation, but it doesn't become a psychological attack until it becomes malicious. In other words, there is a difference between plain old persuasive arguments and using persuasion to carry out dark psychology.

Regular persuasion is the type that might make you vote for a candidate or buy some product (though some would argue that modern-day advertising has dark psychology aspects). On the other hand, malicious persuasion might entice you to go against your set of morals and beliefs. This sort of persuasion is dangerous because an attacker's arguments may seem very convincing to you when, in reality, they are just cleverly designed to trick you. At the same time, the persuasion is being used to benefit someone else.

The dark psychology mindset tells us that there are people out there with less than kind objectives. They may be after your wealth, your emotional labor, your body, your mind, or just a few minutes of your attention. And all of this is theoretically possible through the levying of persuasive techniques. But first, we should talk about everyday persuasion in the traditional sense.

Modern-Day Aristotle

No matter what persuasive argument you come across, they will have all of the semblances of Aristotle's appeals, mixed in with a modern "secret sauce" that is unique to the persuader (and indeed the situation). It is still worth talking about persuasion and persuasive arguments because they are the cornerstone of all manipulation types. If a manipulator were a boxer, persuasion techniques would be like their left jab. Not as powerful as a KO punch, but still the punch that lands them the most points and slows down their opponent.

A modern-day Aristotle can be anyone. A politician, a used car salesman, even your mother is trying to convince you to move closer to home. And it is your job to decide whether their needs are genuine and desirable for all parties. They will no doubt stop at anything to convince you that they are. To do this, you have to separate their argument from the chaff. For persuasive techniques, the chaff is usually the bubbly language or the sharp edge in their arguments that cut you into you.

But beware. Just because it cuts you, it doesn't mean that it is deep or meaningful to you in any way. Many skillful persuaders will only pander to already preconceived notions that their audiences may have. They say something that they know their audience will like and instantly become that much more credible.

But someone trying to come up with a novel argument will first have to design a rhetorical strategy using any of the three rhetorical modes available. It is true whether they are trying to form an essay, a speech, or persuade you into doing something. The world of sales is chock-full of strategies used designed to get you to buy. A competent salesperson may try to get to know you first (especially if the purchase is large, like a new house or car). They wish to form a relationship on a first-name basis and then pose as a close friend.

In the world of sales, the only thing that matters is the purchase. If a client decides to buy, then whatever strategies are used to make that sale are fair. It opens the ground for deploying several different types of psychological tricks against the unsuspecting client. For example, a salesperson may introduce them to a high-end item that is purposely out of their buying range and then redirect them towards an item of similar functionality perceived as being more affordable.

A family looking to buy a new laptop for their college-bound son may be directed towards the expensive and latest Apple laptop product only to realize that it is well out of their budget. The savvy salesperson can then walk them to the Windows computers aisle and show them an alternative product that is the same color as an Apple computer but has a different operating system and is slightly less performative. Now, that other laptop may still be a flagship item and have a sizable price tag, but it is perceived as a good buy by the family because the salesperson showed them an item, they believe to be state of the art.

More psychological persuasion involves more trickery and deception—the type of things one would expect except dark psychology techniques. Indeed, the salesman's trick of going high and then going low can pass as a type of emotional manipulation. It is subtle, but there is clear pandering towards what clients believe their money can buy them. First, they are shown what is considered to be the "it" product. But since they can't afford it, the salesman puts them on an emotional roller coaster of desire.

In a way, it is a projection of what the client believes they deserve. Sure, they can't afford the best, but since they feel like they deserve the best (and since the salesman believes they deserve the best), buying the other best product is an easy choice. And if they can afford the high-end object the salesman shows them first, their job is already finished. In other words, whether the client buys the expensive item or the lesser expensive one, the salesman still wins. It is a perfect example of a psychological manipulation that is difficult to detect in the moment's heat and has a high success rate.

Chapter 5: Models of Persuasion

If you have mastered the art of persuasion, you have garnered a multifaceted and priceless skill. Persuasion is another way of getting what you want without bleeding your victim or target individual completely dry. Successful persuasion is created by building trust between two parties, whether superficial or not, to achieve a specific goal through the act of persuasion.

The core component of persuasion is using persuasive language, a diverse method of using language, language constructs, and, if you prefer a traditional approach, rhetorical devices in speech or conversation as a persuasion method (Lamb, 2013). Although the act of persuasion generally has a singular goal, which is to persuade and get an individual to react in a certain way, there are different types of persuasion, some more sinister than others. Whichever way, it is useful to know the differences between persuasion and manipulation; manipulation has the opposite effect on individuals, which means that you won't get the desired response from your target individual or audience if you confuse the two.

Traditionally, persuasion is classified into three rhetorical categories, which are still used in academic writing today to train students in classic argumentative techniques. These persuasive techniques or rhetorical devices are known as ethos, pathos, and logos. These techniques, which the famous philosopher Aristotle taught over 2000 years ago, still have some relevance in our methods of persuasion today. Let's fly through them before focusing on the darker realm of persuasion. Firstly, ethos refers to a person's credibility when it comes to their persuasive technique. This can include "automatic" credibility that a person would have if they, for example, hold a Ph.D. in a specific field, and they are aiming to persuade you of something within that field. You are likely to believe them without question due to their qualifications, and this is an example of ethos. After, pathos relates to how effectively the attempt to persuade appeals to human emotions. If you can move a person with your persuasive tactics, then you were successful according to the concept of pathos. Finally, logos refer to persuasive tactics that appeal to an audience or a target's rational side. Facts are necessary to establish a basis on which you can build other persuasive tactics. In this case, it's best to avoid faulty logic and prepare this part of your approach, so it comes across as organized and natural ("Modes of Persuasion," 2018). As persuasive tactics developed through time to fit marketing and sales needs, and even other darker requirements, new approaches and methods have been added to ensure a foolproof approach and a high success rate.

Covert Persuasion

Covert persuasion is regarded as one of the most successful persuasive techniques by those who have studied its techniques and potential. The purpose of covert persuasion is not to be unethical or underhanded but to be so subtle that the target individual doesn't notice that these tactics are being used. And, as they say, as subtle as they are, they are also equally effective. Let's take a look at why and how this subtler-than-subtle approach is so deliciously deceptive.

The primary principle of covert persuasion is changing the perception of the "main idea" the target individual has in their mind without them realizing it. Of course, you'd want to gently nudge their ideas into the direction you want it to go, whether it is for them to become more perceptive to buying your products or using your services as a business or just to support your idea from a social perspective. One of your most powerful weapons in covert persuasion is words and how you use them (Gulyani, 2014).

When you use covert persuasion, it's important to be aware of the fact that your target's weak point is their emotions, and this is how the persuasive process starts - by playing on those emotions and steering them into a favorable direction by establishing trust, building rapport, and using words that resonate with your target. However, you can't achieve successful results using covert persuasion if you don't apply yourself to your client's situation and listen to what they say. If you listen and try to rephrase their ideas in your own words and your frame of reference, you'll better understand their point of view, which will give you a head start when it becomes your turn to speak. And, when it's your turn to speak, you can use words wisely to play on the issue you just identified by actively listening to your target. Covert persuasion is also about figuring out what will prevent your target from becoming more agreeable. For example, if you are trying to make a sales pitch to your target, it will benefit your approach if you can identify any past bad experiences they've had with sales or salespeople. You can use this "bad experience" as a tool of persuasion. Here are some of the most important covert persuasion tactics you need to know about whether you are in sales or you want to know how persuasion works so you can identify when it's happening to you (Dejan, 2020).

Persuasion and Manipulation: Know The Difference

The first and very basic indication that there is an elephantine gap between the concept of manipulation and persuasion is how people react when you label them as one or the other. For example, if you call a person a manipulator or a manipulative person, this is generally seen as an insult because people see it as an attack on their character. However, if you call someone persuasive, they may see this as a compliment. So, for some reason, even though persuasion and manipulation have a few things in common, manipulation is regarded to be different from other forms of influence and is also generally considered to be immoral.

Manipulation's bad reputation is most likely linked to its effect on the individual or group being manipulated, in contrast to those subjected to persuasive ethical tactics. As we learned, a victim of manipulation is harmed, mostly emotionally, and even advertisements and marketing can cross the line from persuasion to manipulation. However, we also know that there are instances where manipulation can be harmless, so its sinister quality lies in the intent of the manipulator and not the act of manipulation itself. Let's say, for example, a good friend was in a relationship where she was abused and treated badly, and the relationship subsequently ended. However, she wants to reconcile with her ex, but those close to her know that the abuse would start again if this happens. To alienate their friend from her abusive ex, they tell her that he's been cheating on her in an attempt to make her change her mind about him, which is a dishonest, manipulative act. However, they are doing this to keep her from making the same mistake again, so do you think this is an example of malicious or immoral manipulation? (Noggle, 2018).

On the other hand, while there is a sense of duality linked to the ethics behind manipulation, communication theorists claim that persuasion should be classified as ethically neutral. What does it mean if something is regarded to be ethically neutral? Does this mean that it is or can be good? A useful way to understand the difference between persuasion and manipulation is to view persuasion as a way to align your objectives and views with those of your audience. Persuasion utilizes behavioral insights, but if it is true to its nature, it does not exploit the target audience's psychological and emotional weaknesses. The core difference between the two approaches seems to start with intent (Okoli, 2018).

After taking in all of this insightful information, there is still one dilemma. Why, if some acts of manipulation have good intent, are they still seen as manipulative and not persuasive if the key difference is the intent? The answer here is that these bona fide acts of manipulation, no matter how honorable the intent, still use manipulative tactics like dishonesty and deception, such as in the example earlier, the girl's friends deliberately deceived her by telling her a lie about her ex to protect her from further abuse. It's like comparing two white shirts to each other. One is spotless, and the other has an oil stain but is not completely spoiled.

Persuasive Techniques to Know And Use

The following techniques are squeaky clean. They work, and to master the darkness, you have to know the light. These methods and tips will help you know what to look for, how to read, and what to say to people if you want to persuade them successfully. Let's get you geared up for success.

Start a conversation by actively trying to determine how a person's mind works, what drives them and motivates them. Try to learn about the person you are engaging with and their interests, and if you don't know anything about them, show a genuine interest and fake it 'til you make it. By talking about a topic that interests the person, they will automatically lower their mental defense level. This is a classic covert technique that will help you position yourself in a space where you can connect with the person on a comfortable level. Keep in mind that this position should enable you to create change in this person's way of thinking, and this change should specifically work towards your end goal. It's a great tactic to build rapport with this person; in the end, they must feel better for having met you and feel like they gained something useful or meaningful from talking to you (Nahai, 2013; Dejan, 2020).

When you feel like you've established rapport and a sense of trust you can continue building on, you can use their perspective and motivations, along with factual information relevant to what you want them to believe, to start reframing their mindset. It can be as simple as implying their wants, mentioning the strategic shortcomings of a competitor, and including factual information that will establish a perception of superiority regarding your product in their mind. By doing this, you have created a need for them to choose not just any product, but your product (Musumano, 2017).

Another technique that will subtly imprint certain ideas on the individual's mind is repetition but using it wisely. By mindlessly repeating yourself over and over again, you're going to sound like one of those infomercial ads that want to sell you a dysfunctional vacuum cleaner. You can choose keywords to repeat now and then subtly, and an intelligent approach is to link these words to specific needs the individual has revealed as important to them. For example, when you apply this repetition technique to email writing, you will most likely repeat the same line or similar sentences containing keywords in your subject line, the opening part of your email, and again at the end. Try doing the same when you need to persuade someone. The trick is to make it sound authentic when you are doing it verbally and to not sound like a recording on repeat (Musumano, 2017).

Chapter 6: Manipulation Is Not Evil; It's Just A Tool

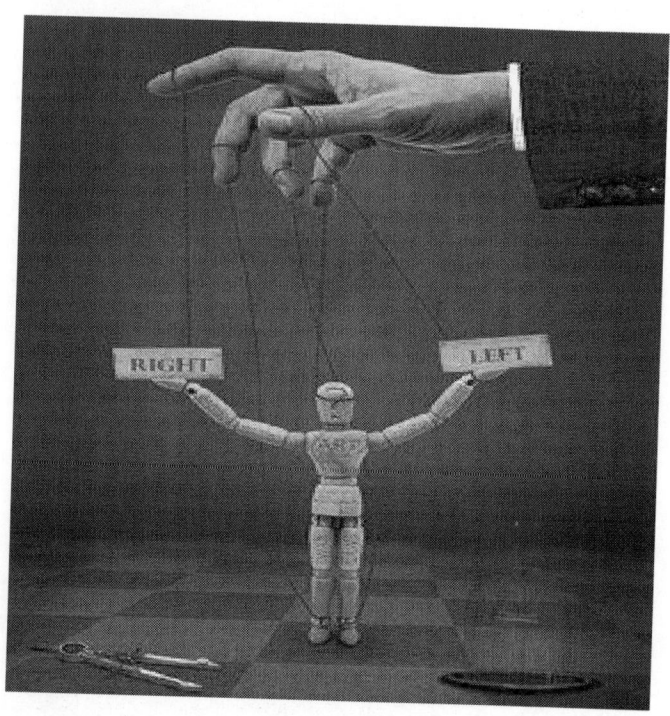

What Is Manipulation?

A speedy check of your word reference would give various meanings of control. In this field, control is depicted as a type of social impact that targets changing the recognitions or practices of different gatherings ordinarily through misleading, injurious, or naughty techniques. All in all, the controller is continually seeking after their inclinations at the person's expense in question. In that capacity, the vast majority of the methodologies they utilize are exploitative, harsh, underhanded, and tricky. Social impact isn't unsafe. However, when the methodology utilized prompts control, it may cause negative results.

When a specialist convinces a customer to change their way of life to defeat medical problems, such as heftiness, we can allude to this social impact. This is an innocuous illustration of the impact. The equivalent applies to all different types of impact whereby the individual is doing the affecting means well for the receptor on the most fundamental level. In actuality, if an individual uses a type of pressure to get their direction and advantage from the receptor's activity or response, this is viewed as a destructive impact and will buy a large amount to control.

Dull enthusiastic or mental control has a few parts of intimidation and influence in it. The parts of intimidation are many, however genuine models incorporate conditioning and tormenting. From a human outlook, these two are beguiling and injurious. The individuals who use control comprehend this excessively well, yet they need to utilize them to impact their casualties. Before the control starts, the controller normally has its ultimate objective in their mind. What remains is to examine the expected casualties and afterward choose the best types of maltreatment to apply in constraining them to achieve them. Coercion is a typical methodology utilized in such occurrences.

A survivor of control may not intentionally cling to the requests of the oppressor. Notwithstanding, they may come up short on any other options, compelling them to allow them their will, contingent upon the strategy used to impact them. Manipulative individuals regularly show an absence of affectability and care towards others; thus, they don't see anything amiss with their activities. An alternate sort of controller just thinks about their ultimate objective and is uninterested in who they hurt in the end route, be it a kid, relative, or dear companion. Most manipulative individuals maintain a strategic distance from solid connections since they dread not being acknowledged. On the off chance that such an individual gets into a relationship, they can't assume responsibility for their issues, practices, and life all in all. What follows is they start the cycle of control and make their accomplices assume control over those obligations.

On the off chance that you examined all types of psyche control, you would understand that a controller can utilize a large portion of them to pick up the impact they frantically need. One of the most widely recognized strategies over the five sorts of psyche control is an enthusiastic shakedown. Here, a controller thinks of an arrangement to summon blame or compassion from their casualty. They see all around very well that blame and compassion are among the most grounded human feelings, which will probably open up their objectives to their control. When their gatekeeper is dropped, the controller exploits the subject and starts the compulsion cycle. Quickly, the subject of control winds up coordinating and helping the regulator in achieving their evil objectives.

One danger of manipulators is that they are not only good at evoking these emotions, but they can evoke them in immeasurable degrees in comparison to the situation at hand. Such a person will make a small situation such as being late to work appear to be as huge as causing a whole company's collapse.

Emotional blackmail is one of many tactics employed by manipulative people. There are others, such as a covert form of abuse known as crazy-making. Just like the name suggests, the manipulator aims to make their subject feel crazy. They create a scenario where the victim develops self-doubt. At times, the self-doubt level might be so severe that the subject might think they are losing their mind. There is yet another form of manipulation where the manipulator acts as if to verbally support their victim but give non-verbal cues that portray contradicting meanings. If they get confronted, they revert to rationalization, justification, deception, and denial to escape trouble.

Another big problem with manipulators is that they might not always be aware of what their subjects need. At times, they might be aware of them but cannot consider and provide them. This does not, at all, justify their behavior. What it does is show that a manipulator will neither consider nor prioritize these needs. They also do not feel any pity, guilt, or shame. The dangerous thing about this trait is that it makes it hard for the manipulator to stop their harmful influence. If this is a point to consider, it explains why some victims of this vice never realize the extent of the damage until it is too late.

Manipulators are also solitary humans. They are most likely to be found alone because they never form or sustain long-lasting relationships. The problem is that after forming relationships of any form, their manipulative nature creeps in and scares their friends or lovers away. People who relate with manipulators confess to feeling used and lacking trust towards the controllers. In this case, the problem affects both parties; first, the controller will not recognize or provide the other party's needs. On the other hand, the affected person will not succeed in creating the emotional connection required to sustain the relations. In the end, both parties go their way, and the manipulator is once again left alone.

The Qualities of A Manipulative Person

According to George Simon, a psychology writer, there are distinct qualities that define a manipulative person. If someone possesses these traits, their chances of being successful manipulators are extremely high. Similarly, if one lacks these traits, they cannot use other people to attain their selfish goals. I bet this is one of those qualifications we all do not want!

In Simon's words, a successful manipulator must:

- Have the ability to hide their aggressive nature and intentions from the public, and more so their potential targets.

- Have the ability to identify the vulnerable aspects of their potential victims to decide which approach to use for efficient manipulation.

- Have an extraordinary level of brutality, which enables them to overcome the qualms that might arise from the harm they cause to their subjects. Ruthlessness can be emotional or physical.

As we can see, the first trait that a manipulator needs to influence other people successfully is the ability to cover up their aggressive intentions and behaviors. Imagine if they went around talking about their dark secrets and plans, nobody would dare to befriend them for fear of being manipulated. The manipulator develops a camouflage that hides their thoughts and plans from other people, ending up appearing normal. Often, the victim walks into the trap with the least suspicion and might not realize it initially. The oppressor will come off as a Good Samaritan, a best friend, or a random person acting sweet. By the time the target becomes suspicious, the manipulator already has enough information to coerce them as they please successfully.

After, the controller must have the skill to observe and determine the vulnerable traits of their victims. This is a typical proverb application that if you must cut down a tree, you better take your time to sharpen your ax. From the identified weak points, they can sit down and decide on the best approach to eating them and effectively attaining their goals. At times, the manipulator will use observation to identify the vulnerabilities, while in others, they need to interact with their subjects for a certain period.

The final trait is that cruelty must be applied. It would be pointless for the manipulator to put in the work required in the above steps to start worrying about what their victims will feel or what will happen to them. If they cared about anyone at all, they would not come up with these plans in the first place. That said, the manipulator puts all the care behind them and ignores any emotional or physical harm that may occur to the victim. To them, what matters is that they achieve their end goals.

From these three traits, we can tell why manipulators succeed most of the time. The amount of planning and trickery that they use is bound to catch anyone off-guard. Due to this, the subject will not be quick to realize that they are in the middle of a manipulative process until the effects begin to show up. They might assume that the oppressor wishes them well, making them drop all defenses. By the time they come to their senses and want to get out, they are already stuck.

Chapter 7: Master Your Emotion is The Key

Many people pride themselves on being rational creatures—after all, humans frequently justify their superiority through rationality, even if that rationality is negligible at best. They like to think that they make decisions based solely upon rationality. However, that cannot be further from the truth.

Do you remember when emotions were mentioned and how they are major motivators for humans? Those same emotions can be tapped into to create the results desired by others. People can frequently be swayed to do certain things or act in certain ways through emotional influence.

What Is Emotional Influence?

Emotional influence refers to the process by which people and corporations appeal to your emotions to sway you to do something.

Perhaps most commonly seen in marketing practices, it works off of the idea that the part of the brain that regulates emotions is also related to decision-making. This makes sense—if emotions are meant to help someone make decisions that will make the individual more likely to survive, it makes sense that the same part of the brain is responsible for processing thoughts.

The way this works is with the theory that the brain works off of dual processing. This means that your brain has two systems that enable it to function—system one, unconscious, meaning it is automatic, nearly instant, and low effort, and system two, which is conscious, meaning it is controlled and takes more effort and is slower.

With the principle of dual processing in mind, you can see that emotions would be regulated by system one while system two would involve rationality and logical decision-making. Between the two, system one, your emotional regulatory area, is always running, which also implies that you are far more likely to make instant, emotional reactions simply because that process is already running in the background of your mind and it requires very little effort or time. Essentially, system one will kick in, make a gut reaction, and then system two will slowly rationalize that decision.

Think about two brands that have been largely seen as rival competitors, where people usually pick a favorite and run with it. It could be whether you are using Apple or Microsoft on your computer, or even whether you prefer cats over dogs. If you are asked which you prefer, you will likely answer one or the other without thinking about it reflexively. This is your emotional system at work. System two, on the other hand, would then kick in, and you would be able to offer the reasoning for that decision.

We think this idea with our emotions first, and rationality following can be particularly useful, especially in dark psychology. If you can appeal to emotion, you can sway the rational side of the brain. If their emotions naturally guide people, you are far more likely to get the results you want if you can sway them one way or another.

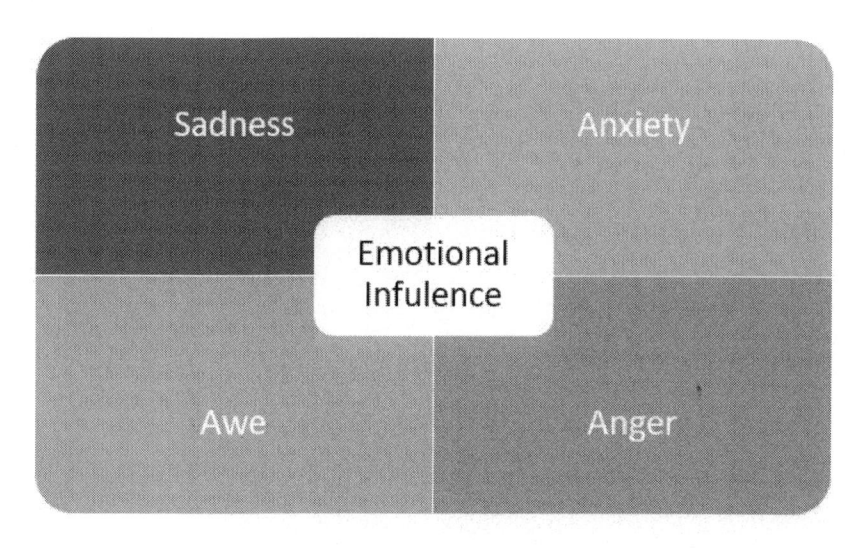

Sadness	Anxiety
Awe	Anger

Emotional Infulence

Principles of Emotional Influence

When looking at emotional influence, four major motivators will sway the decision-making process. All emotions sway decision-making to some degree, but ultimately, these four emotions are the most persuasive. Sadness, anxiety, awe, and anger are the most motivating in terms of inspiring action. You may notice that three of the four are negative—and that is intentional. Negative emotions inspire actions that are meant to avoid them in the future. You want to make the negative emotions stop, and frequently, you may be able to get a reprieve from the emotion based on the decisions you make. For example, sadness can be mitigated temporarily by doing something that you feel stops the cause of the sadness in the first place.

Sadness

Remember—sadness or sorrow is essentially emotional pain. It involves loss, pain, harm, disappointment, or helplessness and implies a need for support and time to heal. It is a negative influencer—it makes you act in ways that will help you avoid feeling sad for that reason again.

Sadness impacts the brain by making the brain function slower. If you are sad, your brain is essentially fogged—have you ever heard the expression "brain fog?" It is felt when sad. The sadness can be overwhelming, acting as a blanket over the person's mental processes and makes decision-making more difficult.

Despite this brain fog, however, people tend to make decisions based on short-term benefits. They want to achieve happiness as quickly and easily as possible, and they will make poor long-term decisions simply to avoid further pain of sadness. They are more likely to undervalue both their actual worth and the worth of other items, as evidenced by people's tendency to price items and services lower when feeling sad than when feeling neutral or happy.

All of this culminates in someone likely to behave impulsively in ways that they think will assuage their sadness. Think of commercials that are meant to make you sad to get you to donate money. They may claim that you are only donating less than a dollar a day, never mind the fact that even offering up $0.50 a day is still going to add up to $182.5 over a single year. While $0.50 in a donation may seem negligible at best, it adds up over time, culminating in a much larger donation over a year that people might hesitate to give in one lump sum. People are more likely to donate those pennies to that sad ad because they want to make the sadness stop, and they feel that offering up the donation would be enough to make it happen.

Awe

Awe is a state of wonder, typically reserved for things that are seen as more powerful or greater than an individual. Typically, people are left in awe of the vast expanse of space, the depth of the ocean, the mystery and daunting task of assembling Stonehenge, or when viewing other similar objects or meeting people that are influential and seen as superior.

When something or someone leaves you in awe, you are more likely to focus on what is happening at the moment. You will feel more aware of what is going on around you but less aware of the passing time. You are in that moment without regard for time, and that focus allows you to appreciate whatever is happening at the moment. This presence at the moment consequently makes people more willing to give. People will be more likely to help others when in awe and are more likely to make decisions that will be more generous than if they felt anxious or afraid.

This is important—you can usually convince someone to do something by first impressing them with something glorious. Think of marriage proposals. For example, they are frequently done with big gestures, such as taking someone on a trip to somewhere breathtaking before proposing. There is a reason for this; people are more receptive when they are in awe. If you take your partner somewhere to propose and you can trigger that awe, you are more likely to get the yes you are looking for.

Anxiety

Anxiety goes hand-in-hand with fear. It is typically an emotion that is felt when anticipating a negative result of something and often is joined by nervous behaviors. For example, if you feel anxious about getting into a car accident, you may have a deep-seated fear of dread every time you enter a car or have a sense that you will die if you get into the car.

When attempting to decide, people who are actively anxious will struggle to read the situation accurately. They will fail to identify cues or context around them, such as recognizing that someone is attempting to manipulate or persuade them to do something that will not benefit the long run. Because anxiety is associated with nervousness, people tend to struggle to identify whether they are in a situation that is stable or that will change shortly, so they struggle.

When feeling anxious, people are particularly receptive to persuasion, and they are far more likely to second-guess their impulses or reactions. It has been found that 90% of those who are actively feeling anxious in the moment are likely to seek advice from other people, whereas only 72% of people are willing to do the same in a neutral emotional state.

Lastly, when feeling anxious, you are more inclined to behave selfishly, simply because you are in survival mode. People in the throes of anxiety are often far more concerned with their feelings than with how others may potentially see them, and because of that, they make decisions that will solve their problems with little regard for the long-term consequences.

Appealing to someone's anxiety can also create fantastic results when attempting to persuade them. Think of a salesperson who wants to sell a newer model car to get a larger commission—she might appeal to the other person's anxiety, emphasizing all of the safety features of the newer model and telling a story about someone who got into an accident in the car that the person is looking at and how the accident did not end well at all. Particularly when used against parents, who only want the best for their children, this can sway people to make decisions that they believe will keep them safer because it helps soothe their anxiety. At the moment, feeling anxious and imagining their children being hurt in the other car, the people are more likely to make the impulsive decision to buy the more expensive, newer car model, even if it is a poor long-term decision.

Anger

Anger is incredibly intense. It spurs you to respond to things aggressively and is often used to protect boundaries that are being perceived as being challenged or violated. It allows you to protect those boundaries, cueing for you to protect yourself in the process. Ultimately, anger is incredibly motivating because of self-preservation instincts.

When angry, people are more successful at recognizing arguments that are weak or strong. They feel more in control and see where things are wrong or weak than strong, compelling arguments. Angry people feel a call to action—they think that something must be changed, and they will work to achieve it. Think of some of the most major social reform that has been accomplished—it is usually around societal issues that instill anger in seeking the change. The people involved were able to clearly and convincingly articulate themselves, which enabled them to make sure the change they wanted to have occurred.

Ultimately, anger can be used to motivate change for that very reason. Suppose people feel as though they have had their rights infringed upon or that something is inherently wrong. In that case, they are more likely to respond with anger, which, in moderation, becomes the most efficient of the emotions in terms of persuading someone to act.

How to Recognize and Overcome Negative Emotions That Control Your Life

We agree that negative emotions are the emotions that make you miserable and sad; the kind that causes you to dislike yourself and other people, taking away your confidence. Depending on the manner you choose to express them and the length of time you allow them to affect you, these negative emotions will dampen the enthusiasm you have for life.

Negative emotions will also keep you from behaving and thinking rationally, from seeing situations through a clear, unbiased lens. When this happens, you see things the way your mind wishes to interpret them, and you remember only what your mind wants to remember. This is a flawed way of viewing and experiencing life because it keeps you from dealing with reality, and the problem with this view of life is that it only prolongs your frustration, anger, and disappointment. Also, the longer you hold on to false beliefs, the more entrenched the prevailing issue will get. On that account, failure to deal with your negative emotions appropriately is harmful.

Recognizing Negative Emotions

The first step to dealing with negative emotions is to recognize and to decode them. To decode an emotion is to slow the emotion or thought process involved, as though you had hit the slow mode on a remote, so that you watch the process frame by frame, systematically, until you find meaning in what is happening.

Most times, when people realize that they are having negative reactions towards other people or a situation, they are often quick to take up measures to reverse their reaction. For example, a wife might say to you, "Tell me what to do to stop being so angry at my husband." Another might say, "What should I do to increase my confidence when speaking in front of a crowd?" From these two popular statements, the people are looking for solutions rather than getting to the root of the problem to understand what could be causing anxiety or fear when speaking in public and what could be the root of the anger felt towards the husband. The reality is that emotions are at the root of all thoughts and actions you take.

The first step towards dealing with the negative situation is to identify the negative emotion that lies underneath. Identifying the actual feeling will provide you with incredible insight into why you are acting the way you do, and therefore allow you to approach the same situation from a different perspective. The principle here is that for you to understand clearly, what you are dealing with, you must first identify the driving emotion.

Below is a step-by-step tactic to help identify and decode your emotions:

Identify the Trigger Thought or Event

Think back to what was crossing your mind when you started feeling as you do right now. It may take a minute to roll back the tape as far back as you can remember. What do you find therein that could have caused your negative emotions? There was likely an event or something that happened to you, something you saw, or an interaction you had with someone that dampened your mood.

From there, now think about the mental response you gave to what happened. Could you have thought that the situation is never going to improve, you are not good enough, you will never succeed, you always take the blame, or that you have had enough? Whatever statement rushed into your mind, take note of it and write it down. Once you have done that, it's time to proceed to step two.

The Emotion or Reaction You Gave

What feeling went with the thought or reaction you gave? Identify the emotions you are having. Is it anger, frustration, fear, loneliness, or pain? (Think along the lines of the emotions we listed in the previous chapter). From the list of emotions, you might identify one or two of those. Write those down, and you can proceed to the third step.

Identify the Physical Manifestation of Your Emotion

What are you feeling in your body, or how is your body reacting to your emotions? Are your fists clenched? Does your face feel hot? Do you have stiffness in your neck or a headache? Is there pain in your stomach? Well, the physical manifestation varies from one person to the other, and there are no wrong answers here. Only take your time to identify how your body may have changed. Besides, you are learning a new skill, and it requires patience and full attention. Once you have identified the said sensation, put it down on paper also.

By now, you have a 'chain' of events listing the negative thought, the emotion you felt, and the reaction or sensation that followed. Let's see an example:

"I am the only one who seems to care" --- Loneliness, Frustration, anxiety --- Headache, Hot Face

Look at what you just did. You unraveled the reason behind your negative emotions. You can correctly identify how you are feeling (lonely, anxious, and frustrated), you know how it is manifesting in your body (a hot face and a headache), and you know the reason why this is happening (people have left you to do something by yourself). You finally have an idea about how your mind works when driven by negative emotions.

Before having this information, how would you have to behave instead of what you are feeling? Chances are you wouldn't have taken time to even determine the feelings running through you. Sometimes, people confuse anxiety, fear, disappointment, and frustration with anger. You would have probably taken up action to fight anger while you were just anxious. You would have behaved in the wrong manner too. However, you now have a vivid description of your emotions and your trigger.

With the information above, will you react differently from how you would have behaved, typically? Do you think you can now make different choices with the information you have got now? The goal of taking time to identify the negative emotions is to slow down your reaction time so that you have enough time to process your mind. That way, your body will give a different reaction.

For example, once you identify the negative thought underlying, your next task is to challenge your thoughts through positive talk and reality testing. For example, you could ask yourself, "Do I complain every time I am asked to do a task by myself?" "Do people react negatively whenever I speak to them?" "Do I patiently request for assistance when I perceive a task as too great for me to do by myself?" or "Am I just a nice and cool person that people keep misconceiving?" The chances are that the answers to questions like these will calm you down and keep you from overreacting.

As for the emotions you have taken note of, the process is not about rushing to solve or numb them; sometimes, you only need to recognize them for what they are. After that, all you have to do is take caution and take care of yourself whenever the emotions arise. For example, whenever you feel alone and fearful, ask a friend to come by, and if at work and you feel like you have been left to handle a difficult task by yourself, ask for some help until when you are comfortable enough to take on the role by yourself. If you have felt angry because of something that was done to you, find a productive way to utilize the extra energy, and diffuse the anger.

Identifying the physical reaction and from where it manifests is important because it allows you to learn how to cope with your emotions and the consequent physical responses before the thoughts and feelings you have to fester or grow into something bigger and unmanageable. As you practice doing this and keenly listening to your body even when you do not have any negative emotions, you will realize that your body gives forth so many messages. These messages are often masked in unhealthy coping habits like shopping, drinking, unhealthy coping, eating, and oversleeping, among others.

For the most part, your mind will be influenced by the state of your body, and when you are unaware of the condition your body is in, you will not understand the feelings, thoughts, and judgments that you come up with. However, as you become better at identifying the physical location of your feelings, you will be able to connect with the respective emotions also. Once you do that, you will start taking measures to take care of your body better, and this could be as simple as taking more breaths, taking deeper breaths, and some stretching to get rid of the physical tension.

Identifying your emotions is the first step to behavioral change, and your thoughts and physical reactions have everything to do with it. When you have control of your emotions, thoughts, and actions, you have control over the influence negative events will have on you. Try to practice the exercise given above as often as you can, and if you are willing to be more vulnerable, you could do it along with your partner, friend, or family member. Discuss with them the various reactions you exhibit because they may have noted a behavioral response you had not given any thought to.

Whichever approach you take up, the point of doing this exercise is to increase or enhance awareness of your emotions and to advance your thought process so you can learn more advanced strategies and patterns to slow and manage your reactions.

As you learn how to manage stressful situations in this new way, compare your progress with how good you did when you did not know this three-step process. See how you have grown and progressed. You will be proud of the person you have become.

Overcoming Negative Emotions

People take up various approaches to overcome their negative emotions. Some opt for diversions, others distractions while others choose to bury the negative emotions, only to realize that they did not move past the feelings they were having, and are still stuck in their negativity. The struggle to move past the negative influences while still being pulled back by the unresolved issues will feel like an internal battle. However, it is possible to overcome negative emotions in the right way.

Research and personal experience will tell you that struggling with, trying to drown out, arguing with, and pushing out the emotions you have only amplifies them and makes them worse. Therefore, as you go through the following steps, keep in mind that there are no quick fixes, and it will take patience, practice, and persistence on your part to achieve the intended goal.

Steps to Take to Overcome Negative Emotions:

Walk away from any negative thought patterns

Patterns are typically repetitive, which means that negative thought patterns allow negative, unhelpful thoughts to repeat themselves. As you would expect, this process yields negative, unpleasant, and unwanted emotions like depression, fear, anxiety, shame, unworthiness, and stress. As such, the key to avoiding negative thoughts is to cut out the negative thought patterns in the first place.

The process of walking back from negative thoughts is called cognitive defusion. Cognitive defusion encourages you to learn to see your thoughts simply as that, like thoughts. You see, when we join our thoughts to our persons, we end up taking the thoughts very seriously, and we believe them, even when they are not true. However, the cognitive defusion state demands that you do not take your thoughts too seriously; you only hold them lightly.

While taking your thoughts very lightly, you only take notice of them when they seem valuable and helpful. In doing this, you should remember that not all your thoughts will be 'truthful' or valuable, which means that you shouldn't follow through or play out each of them. Think of those thoughts as bits of information that pass through the mind every now and then, and you have a choice in how you choose to deal with and respond to each thought.

Let's consider this example: suppose it's on your wedding day and in the morning, you look out the window, and it's raining. What would be the first thought that would rush through your mind when you see the rain? You will think that your day is now ruined. You might say, "What a dreadful day it's going to be." If you think about it, does rain cause an entire day to be ruined? Of course not. Rain is just like any other weather. However, if you go by the thought that the day will be dreadful, you will be stuck in cognitive fusion because that negative thought will have fused with your thoughts, and guess what will await you? A dreadful wedding day. This is to show that whenever you allow your negative thoughts to take control, you are only aiding in the process of generating negativity, to your detriment.

In explaining cognitive defusion, I do not assume that negative thoughts will not come up. They will because they are a part of our daily lives. It is not every day that your life will feel like a fried egg, sunny-side up! Negative thoughts will come up. The problem, however, is not the negative thoughts, but your belief that the thoughts are true. Whenever you disentangle yourself from this kind of negativity, the unpleasant thoughts lose their power and the ability to generate negative emotions.

Now, getting back to our example, suppose that on the morning of your wedding, you looked through the window and saw that it was raining. The negative thought: "what a dreadful day," came up and you only allowed it to float around in your mind, without buying into it. As you continue watching the rain, you also start to see the negative thoughts fall away. In this case, when the thought came up, you did not believe it, did not fuse with it, and did not allow it to generate any emotions in you. Instead, you slide back into a chair or lie on your bed and begin to think how lovely the day will be. You start to rehearse your vows, and you imagine living with the love of your life. All this as the pitter-patter of the rain continues on the roof.

The second scenario shows just how much easier it would be to avoid negative emotions after recognizing unhelpful thoughts. Stepping back can be extremely liberating, and it can change the quality of your day or even your entire life.

Become Aware

From your experiences, you must have noticed that your negative thoughts flow from two distinct directions: dwelling on issues of the past and worrying about what is to be in the future. When you dwell on the past, you mostly ruminate over mistakes, guilt, problems, and issues in the past that did not go as you had hoped they would. On the other hand, people worry about the future because they are afraid of what might or might not happen in the future, for themselves and others.

Negative thoughts, particularly about the future, are common. People worry that they might not achieve particular goals or have anxiety because of their relationships or finances. Others worry that their skins are aging. Others worry that they are not doing as well as their peers. Whatever the negative thoughts of worry are, you will notice that for them to turn into anything substantial, your mind must have been engaging with thoughts of the future or thoughts about the present. For example, if you think your current job is too difficult or underpaying, you are likely to be worried about the future, that you may not be able to sustain your family with the money you are getting. While that may push some people to do something about their current financial situations, most people do not get past the point of worrying.

When you are lost in negative thinking, you become so engrossed in them that you lose touch with what is currently going on in your life. The result is that you miss out on the little joys of today. Have you watched a movie where a spouse was so engrossed in the other's mistake that he or she did not notice the good that his or her partner was doing, and eventually, the accused partner grew tired and walked out of the relationship? You must have. That is how we miss out on the good about the present focusing on the past that we cannot change or the future that we cannot predict. In the end, we end up losing 'partners.'

Instead of obsessing about things, take time to enjoy the sunshine today. Do you feel the taste of the food you are eating? Are you taking time to enjoy the relationships you have with your friends and loved ones? Have you thought about what is good today? Did you notice the sunshine, or the drops of rain falling? There is so much beauty around you; you cannot afford to get lost in your head and lose touch with the world around you or lose touch with who you are.

The way to step out of any negative thinking is to 'come to your senses.' This means that you need to redirect your attention from the thoughts that run through your head and instead, focusing on what your sense perceives presently. Wherever you are, whether in the park, on the subway, at home, or in your office, take some time to notice all that is around you. Engage all your senses, and don't be tempted to involve your mind and start a mental dialogue as you do this. Your goal here is to only be aware of what surrounds you. When you do this, you will be practicing mindfulness. Slowly, your mind and your senses will calm down, be grounded, and be fully aware of your surroundings.

Practice Mindfulness Daily

As we grow and become more taken by our problems, desires, hopes, goals, and dreams, we forget the deep, inborn peace and pure unconditioned inborn awareness that is entrenched deeply in all of us. In this state, it is easy to be so drawn into your negative thoughts that you lose your sense of self.

In reality, your mind is like an ocean on which surface waves will cause great tumult on the surface, yet the depths remain unaffected and peaceful. Inside you perfect stillness, just beneath your thoughts, habits, and conditioning which tend to be tumultuous. Beneath all that is an undeniable quiet that serves as a calm refuge, and it is always available for you.

As such, mindfulness is the ability to get down to that natural wellspring of peace and wholeness. It is the ability to get out of your wondering state so that you can live consciously. Mindfulness allows you to live with that inner peace, to the point that you can gain a deeper awareness and monitor your mind. The result is that you will have decreased stress, anxiety, and depression. It also improves the working of your immune system.

People who practice mindfulness report greater life satisfaction and happiness while those who allow their minds to wander lead unhappy lives.

Distinguishing Helpful from Unhelpful Thoughts

Getting rid of some negative thoughts can be quite difficult, resisting both the identification and the mindfulness approach. If you are in a situation like this, and you discover that some thoughts are 'sticky,' there remains an approach you can take to untangle yourself from your thoughts. This approach involves asking yourself some helpful questions to challenge unhelpful thoughts and redirect your focus.

Some of the questions you should give some answers to include:

Is the thought helpful or unhelpful?

If yes, am I sure that it is helpful?

Are these thoughts coming up out of habit?

Do your thoughts make you take some effective action?

The questions above will help you determine whether your thought ought to be left alone to die or whether you should attend to it. Once this is done, you should now focus on the questions below to see if you can find a new focus or some new possibilities. These questions will help you shift to some creative actions and thoughts and enable you to face daily challenges more effectively so you can have a more meaningful life.

They include:

What is the underlying truth in this situation? Where do I truly stand on this issue?

How do I expect the situation to play out, and how can I work towards that?

How best should I handle this situation?

How would my life play out if these negative thoughts did not come up?

How can I see this situation from a different angle?

What new thought or story should I now focus on?

How much more can I be grateful for the moment and my surroundings?

Once you answer the questions above, you will be on the path to changing your focus from being stuck in negativity to focusing on what is going well. This way, you can also take on constructive action and make your life more meaningful.

Chapter 8: Key Elements of Persuasion

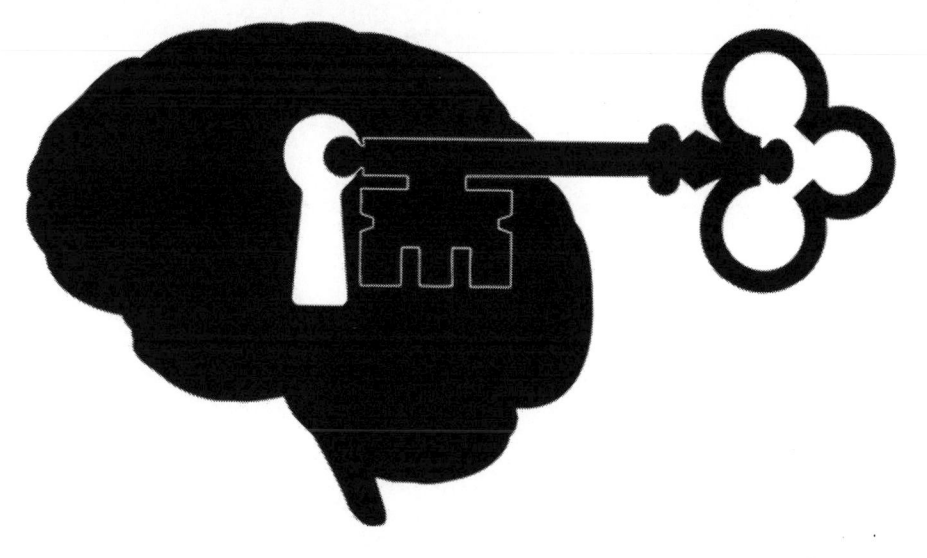

Persuasion is the ability to transmit ideas and disseminate them by those who act as recipients. This translates more effectively as the ability that human beings have through a relationship, to convince others. Persuasion is a tool that can be used in fields such as marketing, advertising, and commerce, basically sectors of the economy in which the public is sensitive to various interactions with environmental media and where the decision is the objective of who persuade

Let us elaborate on a scene where a seller wants his products to be acquired by the buy. Besides being useful, l must be attractive and, in one way or another, more desirable than that of the competition. This is achieved with persuasion, which attracts customers by offering the best product or service attributes, effectively providing comfort to the buyer by relating the most promotional aspects to the most personal. In turn, persuasion generates competition and demand in the market, generating dynamism of intentions and offers that fosters sustainable economies.

Another use of persuasion that we see in a society constantly is in the application of the law. In a trial, the lawyers and the law, as the main tool, use the elements in their favor and persuade the jury and the judge that they are valid to win the case.

We are always waiting for others who live in our environment to reproduce or share our ideas. Even unintentionally, people seek to persuade others so that their ends are fulfilled. A wife who asks her husband to optimize expenses is trying to convince him that it is the best for both. Either way, each person's ideas will be interpreted as an intention for others to apply and build their ideas based on the initial idea. Persuasion can be so extreme that it can change how a person thinks; it all depends on what the person who persuades another looks like.

To better understand the process by which one person or medium can influence another by changing their mind, it is necessary to take into account the key elements of the process, these being the issuing source, the receiver, the message itself, and the technique that It is used to transmit it.

1. **Issuer**

Concerning communicating the data, the source that attempts to convince, two qualities are mulled over regarding being or not being convinced: its appeal and believability. It has appeared in different investigations that we, by and large, consider those people we see to be more solid (incompletely in light of the radiance impact, in which we accept that somebody who has a decent quality will have others). These are the reasons why people of incredible actual allure, or all-around esteemed VIPs, regularly show up in promoting to sell us an item.

Nonetheless, the most compelling component of the source regarding convincing us is believability, which is given to the source's degree of skill in the topic and the apparent genuineness.

2. **Receiver**

As to the beneficiary of the message, the principal qualities that influence the hour of being affected are simply the degree of knowledge, regard, and contribution to the subject.

It must be contemplated that the knowledge level's impact ought not to be taken as an immediate measure. It isn't that who is more powerful is less astute, yet somebody with higher knowledge will have more assets to scrutinize the contentions set forward in influence. By having a higher ability to learn and use the data continuously retained, exchanging the most intelligent individuals is more liquid and reliable, reflected in the outcomes they acquire regarding persuading.

Concerning confidence, we, by and large, find that the lower confidence, the more outlandish we will think about our contentions as substantial, all the more effectively tolerating those of others.

3. **Message**

One more of the fundamental components with regards to convincing somebody is simply the message. A few investigations show that the reality of utilizing a more normal or more passionate message will rely upon the kind of reaction you need to support. It likewise influences the message consolidating components that cause dread or a feeling of danger: as indicated by Rogers's security inspiration hypothesis, we will, in general, look for and consider more certain words that permit us to limit or maintain a strategic distance from harm.

The way that influences frequently happens with a shut or open message has been examined, showing that it is commonly better to leave an end not entirely clear, albeit guided toward which one wishes to convince. This might be because this way, the audience members are more fulfilled when they arrive at those resolutions, something they experience as though it had been a revelation made without anyone else, without somebody attempting to force a thought from outside.

Chapter 9: Persuasion Skills

First, you need to learn to recognize when you are being manipulated so you can counteract it. For this purpose, we will now look at what the experts say on how this sort of behavior can exist among us.

Are you feeling manipulated?

What then, in our everyday lives, do we need to be wary of?

Persuasive Language

The idiom that every picture tells a story is very true. Words can be so much more powerful as they inspire and encourage us, even to the point of manipulation. How many times have you been inspired by a good orator, whose daring speech motives you into action? Words even influence when we are lost completely in a great journal. The art of words can influence us to believe something, even when our eyes tell us differently. Communication is a powerful tool, especially when it comes to making people do things.

Six Theories of Psychological Manipulation

Cognitive

There are many well recognized psychological processes in theories regarding the art of persuasion. One of those is the Cognitive Response model, developed by Anthony Greenwald in 1968. It is still relevant today for determining some factors in persuasion. It is also a model used extensively in the world of advertising.

Greenwald suggested that:

It is not the message that determines the success of persuasion, but more the receiver's emotions. The internal monologue of the one receiving the message will decide how easily they are influenced. Such internal thoughts will include positive and negative aspects, according to the individual's personality. This not a learning process, but more based on whether the person already views the message with favorable or unfavorable thought processes (cognition).

Overcoming any counter-arguments will rely on the expertise of the persuader. They should stop their target from having sufficient time to construct any counter-arguments. The persuader must encourage positive arguments to come to the forefront. This gives the "persuasion effect" a better chance of success.

Persuasion can be more difficult if the intended target has been forewarned. It allows the target time to build counterarguments if the "message" is counter-intuitive to their present cognitions. The importance of pre-warning can be seen in research conducted by Richard E. Petty in 1977. The study showed that students given notice about a certain event were less likely to be persuaded than those who had no pre-warning.

Reciprocity

Another well-studied explanation for how we might be open to the power of persuasion is the Rule of Reciprocity. This is based on a principle related to social conventions. If someone does you a favor or does something good for you, you will be more likely to feel obliged to return the favor.

The Rule of Reciprocity can also happen subconsciously. Without even realizing it, you may agree to action, or favor asked of you by the requester. All because at some point, they had done something for you, and you feel in their debt. You may feel obliged even if the request is something you would normally decline.

It is an effect widely used by companies who are looking to make sales. Often companies give out free samples or time-limited trials. This is not without a motive. It is hoping that the customer feels obliged to return the favor and buy the product or continue with the agreement.

Reciprocity is a recognized psychological process. It is an adaptive behavior that would have increased our chances of survival in the past.

By helping others, it is likely that at some following point, they will help you. However, it can also have negative effects. If someone does something bad to you, you may be driven by reciprocity rules to exact your revenge.

The Rule of Reciprocity is well supported by academic research. Burger et al. (2009) suggested that a group of participants were more likely to agree to a request if the requester had partly done them a favor.

Information Manipulation

A powerful tool in the manipulator's armory. This is a method of being outright deceitful. It is a means of providing limited and confusing information to the victim. The effect of this will unbalance their way of thinking, making them vulnerable. It can also incorporate the use of intentional body language to persuade and manipulate someone.

A study by McCornack et al. (1992) showed the different ways a message can be falsified to assist in the manipulation process. McCornack's theory has a premise of four maxims in a truthful statement. A breach of any of these will render the message as intentionally deceitful. The four maxims are:

Quantity

This is the "amount" of information provided. Most of us seek to provide the right amount of information so that the receiver understands our message. Not too little, or too much, as that might confuse. A manipulator, though, would play with that quantity of information. They may omit certain pieces they consider irrelevant most, especially if it is likely to work against their argument. This is known as "lying by omission."

Quality

Refers to the "accuracy" of the information provided. Truthful communication is one of High Quality. If we were to violate this maxim, then the receiver hears intentional mistruths. This is "outright lying" to gain the manipulator's power.

Relation

Here, we talk about the "relevance" of the information to the message. To confuse or sidestep an awkward question, the manipulator may go off-topic. This is a way of changing the subject for the sole purpose of misleading. It could be to hide their weaknesses. Or even to over-emphasize something that will give them more power over their listener.

Manner

The "presentation" of the message. An important aspect of this is body language. We read inflections and facial expressions as we listen. A manipulator may exaggerate these to mislead the presentation of the message. This is all in the aim to emphasize their agenda.

Lying to manipulate or persuade someone is not a new concept. It is, though, a method that is becoming particularly potent in the modern world. Online communication and social media do not always involve face-to-face contact. This makes it easier to tell mistruths or exaggerate information. A manipulator may work in their elements with such communications.

Nudge

Not all manipulation is sinister. Sometimes we may be manipulated to help us make the right decisions for our good. To do this, the Nudge Theory is particularly useful. The Nudge Theory expands positive reinforcement by using small nudges.

Skinner's studies, or behaviorism, show how useful this theory can be. Positive reinforcement, such as rewards, can manipulate people into behaving in the manner you are hoping to encourage.

One example of "nudging" can be seen in this example. Adding exceptionally high-priced items on a menu may seem counterproductive. Yet, the result of this increased the sales of the second highest-priced item. The customers were given a "nudge" in the right direction, but for the restauranteur's benefit.

Richard Thaler, considered the Nudge Theory father, was awarded the Nobel Memorial Prize in Economic Sciences. His contribution to behavioral economics was considered quite momentous. Nudge Theory gives positive reinforcement, or as Thaler described it, it gives "nudges."

The Nudge Theory is not only effective in economics. It can be used to encourage behavioral changes and to influence personal choices. Even accepted social norms can be manipulated to changes in this way.

Nudging is so successful that in 2010 the British Government set up a Department Behavioral Insights Team. This was to help develop policies. The department was referred to as the Nudge Unit.

There can be obvious benefits of using "nudges" to influence people. It is still a form of psychological manipulation that can infringe on an individual's civil liberties.

Social Manipulation

This type of manipulation is also known as psychological manipulation. It is often a tool for politicians or other powerful people who are used to advancing their interests. In its worst form, it is a means of social control. By taking away individuality, it coerces the populace into accepting what is given to them. Though it can have a positive side when used to help with personal issues, such as improving health and wellbeing.

Those in power who use social manipulation may use destructive techniques to deflect from important issues. They would argue that their proposals are for the benefit of the populace and the benefit of your family and its future. Anything you think personally that might be different is wrong and selfish. This type of persuasion is very paternalistic, almost treating individuals as if they were all children. This "system" will strive to make the crowds believe the things that have gone wrong are, in fact, their fault. The only way to resolve the problem is to listen to the guidance of those who know better.

Such a political strategy would bring to the forefront one social problem, only to hide another. It is a tactic to cause social unrest and panic among the populace. By creating unease in society, the populace will begin to demand changes. An example could be that the department wishes to hide the problems of health care. So, they decrease the budget in crime prevention, causing crime statistics to rocket. The populace will receive information to coerce them into believing the best way forward for the crime problem. The politicians will feed propaganda by disseminating their truths and facts. It may not always be true, or it may be information that is exaggerated, such as misuse of statistics. This type of social manipulation could take years to get the result that the manipulator requires.

The use of psychological manipulation is all a part of social influence. Professor Preston Ni, Communication Studies, published an article in Psychology Today. He indicates that one party recognizes another's weaknesses. They deliberately set out to cause an imbalance of power. This enables them to exploit their victims for their agenda.

Gaslighting

This is perhaps the cruelest form of manipulation. It is a means of casting into doubt the sanity and self-esteem of a person. You could say it is sowing the seeds of doubt into the victim of manipulation. Working on a similar principle such as "knowing you are being told repeated lies." Until eventually, you begin to believe the lies as the truth.

It is an unkind form of manipulation. The gas-lighter will cause their victim to lose all confidence in their credibility. This leads to destroying their self-worth. All because they begin to doubt themselves. That is the intention of gaslighting to reduce the victim to a psychological mess. The manipulator will constantly put their target down by contradicting them. Also, by convincing them that they are always wrong. Sometimes to the point that the victim will be accused of telling lies. This is why the victim loses all self-esteem. When that happens, they become ruled by the domineering influencer. It is a form of mental abuse, often seen in abusive personal relationships. The influencer will use constant techniques to make their victim doubt. Even to the point of doubting their memories by denying things they've said and done.

Chapter 10: How to Influence People?

Brainwashing

Brainwashing doesn't come easily and could take quite a lot of time to be effective. This phase is most likely to concentrate on the procedure of indoctrination as well as all the elements that feature it. Many individuals see persuading as a wicked method done by those attempting to corrupt, impact, and get power with the media and the flicks seen.

Some that rely on the power of indoctrination think that individuals around them are attempting to regulate their minds and habits.

Generally, the indoctrination procedure takes place in a far more advanced method and does not include the threatening methods most individuals connect with. This phase will certainly enter into a lot of even more information concerning what indoctrination is and how it can affect the topic's mindset.

Hypnosis

Hypnosis is the after a type of dark psychology I'll be revealing. There are a whole lot of definitions of what hypnosis is. The American Psychological Association explains hypnosis as a supportive interface where the hypnotist provides suggestions to which the participant can respond. However, it becomes dark psychology when the hypnotist starts making suggestions that can harm or change the participant's acts in their environs.

Most people who undergo hypnosis allude it to a sleep-like trance kind of state. However, the hypnosis participant is in vivid fantasies, sensitive suggestibility, and focused awareness. This new-fangled state makes them more vulnerable to the recommendations that the hypnotist supplies them with.

Nonetheless, most experts agree that the effect of hypnosis as a part of dark psychology is not a reality. Although it is possible to convince the mind to accept a few changes in the subject, it is not likely that the subject can change their whole thinking system through this system.

Many certified psychological professionals use this medium to assist the subject towards pain management and self-improvement rather than controlling their minds.

Manipulation

One of the top-ranking types of dark psychology that can control how a person thinks is manipulation. Psychological manipulation is a type of social influence that works to influence the decision of others. It embraces an abusive, underhanded, and deceptive approach to advance the interest of the one manipulating and those being manipulated. While most people recognize when they have been manipulated, they fail to realize that it is a kind of mind control. Manipulation could be very difficult to do away with since it occurs between people who know each other very well.

Manipulations cause the subject not to have a choice in a matter. Their minds are laced with half-truth and outright lies that leave them oblivious of the whole situation until it becomes too late. When they detect things ahead of time, they are being blackmailed by the agent to get their goals finally. The subject remains stuck in between the matter because they'll take the blame eventually if things go haywire.

Persuasion

Another form of dark psychology that works similarly to manipulation is persuasion. This part influences the motivations, behaviors, intentions, beliefs, and attitudes of the subject. Persuasion could be used for various things in our everyday life to affect a necessary form of communication to get people with contradictory ideas to agree. During this process, either spoken or written, words are used for conveying reasoning, feelings, or information to the other party.

There are a lot of different kinds of persuasion that are available. They don't all have an evil intent; however, they all work to change the subject's mind about something. A political candidate comes on TV to try to make the voter or subject vote for a particular person on the election day. The TV or online advert tries to make a subject buy a particular product. These are all types of persuasion bent on changing the thought pattern of the subject.

Deception

Deception can be considered a form of dark psychology that influences the subject's beliefs with either untrue or partial truths about things and events. However, deception could be anything ranging from propaganda, dissimulation, hand sleight, distractions, concealment, or even camouflage. Deception is a serious type of a dark psychology system that could be overly dangerous to the victim, as he or she might not be aware of the dark psychology that is going on. The victim is convinced beyond every necessary doubt that what is being said is nothing but the truth, while the opposite is the case. Deceit could be more dangerous should the concealed information be liable to make the subject prone to danger.

However, the moment the subject starts detecting or detects the agent's motive as deceit all along, they start having trouble trusting that person in future dealings. Nonetheless, deception isn't always laced with evil motives. It could be targeted at keeping a relationship from breaking off.

Chapter 11: Methods of Persuasion

idea — planning — strategy — success

Win-Win Concept

When discussing persuasion, it is important to describe the win-win concept, which can be translated with the expression "win I - win you" put in place by the persuader. It indicates that both sides achieve a goal that both will benefit from in a situation. It is a concept behind persuasion. This is the case of honest sellers who explain the fundamental characteristics of the product they want to sell, which will serve the person who wants to sell it. "You buy this spacious and sturdy machine that you need for your work and your large family, and I make money." They both get something, and nobody loses!

We also find persuasion on TV in commercials, for example, which is made to attract our attention and change our minds about a specific type of product or service. This also happens outside the TV screens; we can see it on billboards or in shop windows while walking around the city.

Build Your Trust

You can't pretend to master the art of persuasion unless you're sure of yourself, what you're doing, and what you're saying. Your audience needs to be able to sense your safety. How can you expect someone to believe what you're saying if you have doubts about it yourself? No matter how competent you are, if your target audience doesn't perceive your safety, you will most likely lose the fight and be unable to convince them.

Intensity

The word 'intensity' in this case refers to verbal language. A study has shown that subjects subject to speeches containing "strong" words, used to support the description of a product or service, are more inclined to purchase that product. This concept is also very valid in political speeches to gather more consensus among the voters. Using strong language is one of the most effective persuasive strategies that exist.

To Select

You have to select the people to reach with persuasion by identifying those interested in our goal and letting go of those who would not get involved because spending time trying to persuade these people would mean wasting time. This is especially true for marketing when you need to target the public.

Mystery

Creating a little suspense always helps persuade because it is very curious, be it, man or woman. For example, if you want to convince your friend to go to a new place, you can intrigue him. They will almost certainly follow you.

Shortage

This is a very effective technique for selling a product. Making people believe that an article is present in small quantities leads them to buy it.

Perceived Value

This, too, like the past ones, is a technique widely used in marketing. In short, it consists of persuading the customer that what he should buy is worth more than the actual value of it.

Be A Good Person

It consists of accompanying the persuasive action with a beneficial action, that is, with something that produces help for someone else. This is because doing good often produces a sense of happiness.

Make It Clear What They're Missing

This persuasive technique leverages fear, in this case, the fear of losing something, and is obtained by showing the potential buyer what he risks losing if he does not buy a product or service.

Be an Observer

You can't go anywhere if you don't pay attention to the surrounding environment, the situation, or, above all, the person you're trying to persuade. Mood, behavior, and situation must be appropriate for the time being for makeup to be effective. Remember how to read body language and know how to read this person before manipulating him into anything. If you are not paying attention to the passion and attention needed to make the trick work, you will be captured, and your success is unlikely. Attention and observation are the keys to manipulation.

Honesty and Reliability

Nobody will follow the advice or suggestions of someone they don't trust. Even if the situation does not require a relationship or a pre-developed relationship, you must appear reliable. Remember the indicators of discomfort and lying when it comes to body language and avoid them when you speak. If you are half-telling the truth or even lying to get what you want from someone, you can't do it by holding your hands behind your back and shifting the weight from one foot to another.

Get Over Your Idea

A tactic often used in the sales sector is to use intense passion to promote the idea which you want to sell to someone. It is a common practice seen by anyone who tries to sell a product, and it works. If you want someone to donate to your favorite organization, tell them that they will benefit as much as the organization will help. Prepare them to follow them before they even know what you want to offer. This technique works well when you want someone to take something, which is why it is taught to all salespeople and used in advertisements. It also works well with the opposite technique, which oversimplifies the idea.

Oversimplify Your Idea

If the idea is complicated and has disadvantages, it may be helpful to oversimplify it. By definition, excessive simplification consists of leaving out information and simplifying what is included until it is distorted. To do this via persuasion, edit what you should explain when it comes to your idea.

Put Yourself in A Neutral Position

If possible, maintain the illusion of neutrality and limit any perceived prejudice. For example, if your friend's girlfriend begged him to cut his hair for a while, then look at you for a second opinion, you shouldn't express any real interest. If you have an issue with his hair's length, you could say that you don't care in both cases. However, the length indicated in his girlfriend's photo would frame his face well, and in the after hot climate, he will avoid the possible stroke heat. The use of words with specific reactions helps. In this case, the word "anyway" causes people to focus more on what was said after than what was said before. By introducing logical points and acting as if your opinion was completely for no reason, your friend will likely choose the hairstyle, and his girlfriend may even owe you a favor.

Change the Environment to Your Advantage

Studies have shown that the environment someone is in can have an impact on their decisions. This would come as a form of subliminal persuasion. For example, if you desperately need a study partner for an upcoming exam, you shouldn't ask your favorite partner in the mall. The mall is surrounded by fun activities, bright lights, music, and other distractions. However, if I asked him in an environment that stimulates the idea of studying in his brain, such as the library, he is more likely to agree with you.

Speak Quickly

If you get involved in a discussion that you plan to win, speed up your speech. If you speak quickly, you seem more prepared with the arguments, and your opponent has less time to think about a coherent answer since he focuses on countering your arguments instead. The other person will fidget and confuse their points. Eventually, they will drop their share of the disagreement out of frustration, and you will emerge victoriously.

Creating Needs

One of the best methods of persuasion is to create a need or to reassure an old need. This question of need is related to self-protection and compatibility with basic emotions such as love. This technique is one of the biggest trumps of marketers in particular. They try to sell their products or services using this technique. The kind of approach that expresses the purchase of a product to make one feel safe or loved is part of the need-building technique.

Touching Social Needs

The basis of touching social needs is popular, having prestige, or having the same status as others. Advertisements on television are ideal examples of this. People who buy the products in these advertisements think they will be like the person in the advertisement or be as prestigious. The main reason why persuasion techniques such as touching social needs are effective is related to television advertising. Many people watch television for at least 1-2 hours a day and encounter these advertisements.

Use of Meaningful and Positive Words

Sometimes it is necessary to use magic words to be convincing. These magic words are meaningful and positive. Advertisers know these positive and meaningful words intimately. They need to be able to use them. The words "new," "renewed," "all-natural," and "most effective" are the most appropriate examples of these magic words. Using these words, advertisers try to promote their products, making the advertisements more convincing for people to like the products.

Use of Foot Technique

This technique is frequently used in the context of persuasion techniques. The processing method is quite simple. You make a person do something very small first because you think they can't refuse it. Once the other person has done so, you will try to get him to do more, provided he is consistent within himself.

Use of Orientation from Big to Small

The tendency to ask from big to small things is the exact opposite of the technique of putting a foot in the door. The salesperson makes an unrealistic request from the other person. Naturally, this demand doesn't correspond with the real issue. However, the salesperson then makes a request that is smaller than before. People feel responsible for such approaches, and they will accept the offer. Since the request is small, by accepting it, people have the idea that they will help the salespeople, and the technique of moving from big to small requests works.

Use of Reciprocity

Reciprocity is a term for the mutual progress of a business. When a person does you a kindness, you feel the need to do him a favor. This is one example of reciprocity. For example, if someone bought you a gift on your birthday, you would try to pay back that gesture. This is more of a psychological approach because people don't forget the person who does something for them, and they try to respond accordingly.

For marketers, the situation is slightly different from a human relations point of view. Reciprocity takes place here in the form of a marketer offering you an interim extra discount or "extra" promotion. You are very close to buying the product introduced by the marketer you think is giving a special offer.

Limitation Technique

The restriction technique is one of the most powerful methods to influence human psychology. You can see this mostly in places selling products. For example, if a store has a discount on a particular product, it may limit it to 500 products. This limitation can be a true limitation or a part of the limitation technique. So, you think that you will not find the product at that price again and you agree to buy that product at the specified price.

Chapter 12: Principles of Persuasion

Reciprocity is one of the major forms of persuasion. It is about the feeling of needing to return something when something is given to you. If you invite someone over to your house, they will feel the need to invite you to their home afterward. When you compliment someone, you can see that people will normally compliment you as well.

If you want to get something from someone else, try to offer them something similar first. It can be as simple as trying their food at a restaurant. After a time, the server brings out two plates, offering your date a bite of your dish. They will likely end up offering you a bite as well.

Scarcity is the second principle. If you make yourself unavailable, then you will become even more desired. Scarcity is a tactic that many people use for online dating. They think that if they rarely respond, they will make themselves more desirable, and the other person will try even harder to mend the relationship. This result is certainly true in some cases, but people will get bored and move along, so make sure you are still giving the people what they want.

Think of one of your favorite brands. At one point in time, the company probably came out with a "limited edition" item. This release is more often than not just a marketing tactic to try and get many buyers all at once. Sometimes limited-edition items become popular enough that they become staples, and the company probably just used the "limited" status as a way to test out their product.

Scarcity is also used when people say that they only have a few items or spaces left. If you are a hairstylist, you might tell your clients to make their appointments quickly because you only have a few spots open. Many people will feel the pressure to schedule, so they will make an appointment even though they might not have been considering doing so partly. If you want to be persuasive, try using this tactic to help you get what you want.

Authority is important in persuasion, but it cannot be confused or misconstrued. Some people assume that authority comes with power and that power equals strength. Many people will yell, scream, fight, and be angry in an attempt to look as though they have authority over others. This tactic can work, but not in a respectable way.

In terms of persuasion and influence, authority refers to someone's credentials. A person will use their past certifications, training, college degrees, and other forms of quantifiable authenticity to prove their credentials. You will hear people say, "I'm a doctor," when describing a health product, which gives them the authority to decide that it is good for your health.

You will often see kinds of toothpaste marketed as "the toothpaste your dentist uses" or something along those lines as an attempt to give authority over your decision. If you want to use this persuasive principle, try finding what your authority might be. If you are interviewing for a position, you might mention that you are a college graduate or a pre-med student to help remind those who hold more power than you do to have a level of authority.

Consistency is crucial for anyone who wants to have persuasion over others. We have already talked about consistency for other reasons, but it is important to know that it is crucial to becoming a persuasive individual.

Consistency is a good skill to have because it makes people comfortable with you. If you are erratic, it can make you seem unapproachable, unrelatable, and somewhat scary.

To use consistency as a form of influence, ensure that you are sticking to your morals, beliefs, and overall identifying factors. Also, find a balance so that you do not become too predictable. If you become a too predictable person, you will not have as much influence over people, resulting in less persuasion.

Being liked is an important aspect for those who want to be persuasive. The most liked people are those who give compliments, cooperate, and are relatable. Figuring out how to be liked is challenging, and it is something that triggers us back to junior high when we were hoping not to be the last call when picking teams.

Being liked as an adult can be easier because most of us are more forgiving and less judgmental and harsh than we were in our younger years. The most liked people are those who are complimentary. However, you do not want to be someone who gives people compliments too often. It can make you seem desperate for approval, which will make you less trustworthy and not as talented in persuasion.

Still, compliments help win over the other person. Make sure your compliments are natural. Do not just give compliments because you are trying to be persuasive, or people will catch on and call you out for your phony behavior.

Others like people who can cooperate. If you show that you are willing to help out, people will be much more likely to listen to you. When you can collaborate and compromise with many different people, it shows that you are someone with whom it is easy to get along, which will lead you to become a person who can easily influence others. When you are relatable, you seem more approachable as well.

For people who are the biggest influencers, relatability is huge. Those you are trying to persuade want to see themselves in your shoes. When they can look at you and find moments of connection, they will be much easier to persuade.

When it comes to persuasion, the consensus is the last thing others will consider. They will make as many informed decisions as possible on their own, but when all else fails, they will look at what everyone else thinks before making their final decision.

For businesses, people will go online and look at reviews to determine if they want to give you their money or not. On a more personal level, people might ask their friends if they know you to get a sense of whether they should like you. Though it is important to connect with the person you are persuading, to be a good influencer, you also want to make sure that the consensus agrees on your likability and credibility.

The Concepts That Make It Work

The amplification theory is another concept that allows persuasion to work. If you build something up, people are more likely to be persuaded. This technique can work if you amplify something negatively as well.

Making someone feel bad about something they like to prove your point or give yourself validation can work, but why would you want to use this strategy? You will initially influence people, but if you continue to make others feel bad about their decisions, they will eventually look to someone else.

Asking for something small is another good concept in helping you get what you want following. If you want to persuade someone to let you borrow a hundred dollars, for example, you might first ask if you can borrow twenty. It is as if you have eased them into asking for the bigger favor following on.

Alternatively, ask for something so ridiculous that they say yes to your second request. If you ask them to dog sit for a month, many people will oppose the thought. If you then ask them to dog sit just for the weekend, they are much more likely to say yes.

Anchoring is a technique that makes someone else think they are getting away with a great deal. Stores like Kohl's and Macy's seem like they are always having some sort of sale. They use anchoring as a method to get you to buy their clothes. Stores plan sales because they know that the illusion of saving money is what gets people to spend their cash.

You can use this method of anchoring as a persuasion tactic as well. When working with a client, if you know it takes you five days to complete a project, you might tell them you need seven. That way, you work hard to get it done in four days, and they are impressed.

In persuasion, relatability and unity are also important. We look at celebrities and wonder where their level of relatability is. Ultimately, they seem like they are perfect, but the top influencers are the ones who are not afraid to be vulnerable.

They will show pictures of themselves, not looking at their best, or share moments when they feel a little down to seem more relatable to their fans. They still don't share all the dirty details, but they have given enough away to keep people coming back because they seem so relatable.

Chapter 13: The Ultimate Guide to Enhance your Persuasion Techniques

The energy of persuasion can open doors for you and develop the road to good results much smoother. Probably the most effective methods have the origins of their NLP (neuro-linguistic programming). These persuasion methods are derived from empathy - to persuade someone - you have to comprehend them.

Empathy-Based Persuasive Techniques

The very first and most significant thing you have to comprehend about the individual you're attempting to influence is precisely what the brain of their best response to - feel, visual, or maybe auditory stimulation.

Knowing this can enable you to be persuasive by plugging into and feeding this particular desire.

Females generally respond better to feelings. However, not. Guys frequently respond very well to visuals, and several individuals are impacted by audio. To discover, and that is the very best stimulation to focus on your persuasion, look at the way they talk. Can they say, "I see," "I hear what you are saying," or maybe "I feel that."? These are obvious examples; of course, the appropriate answer might be far more subtle and maybe a blend of two kinds of stimulation.

Alter the persuasion methods of yours depending on the mind type you're offering; for instance, when persuading somebody who's "feel" orientated, focus on how they will feel if they do what you're attempting to persuade them to. Do not attempt to tell them just what it will be like - you've to make them believe it. The more you are conscious of the individual you are coping with, the more efficiently you will focus on your persuasive strategies.

Mirror Based Persuasive Techniques

Matching the body language of yours, as well as your pose/position, is a subtle but amazingly effective persuasive method. You have to be subtle, which might feel uncomfortable initially; however, with a bit of exercise, you will see just how helpful this particular method, referred to as "mirroring," may create a rapport easing persuasion.

Along with focusing the content of your persuasion in a means that interacts nicely with the specific character style of theirs, you can also correct your language and how you talk to place yourself on the Stage of theirs. Individuals react much better to persuasive strategies that are in their own "language" of theirs. Pick up on certain words they utilize as well as add them back on them, particularly adjectives. Consider their response, volume, pitch, and speed as similarly as you possibly can.

Other Persuasive Techniques

You will find a lot of different persuasive methods that you can focus on and build up. We suggest you learn the empathy/mirror effective methods, most notably, as these are the best. Nevertheless, the following methods may be useful additions to the persuasion armory yours.

- **Persuasive Words**

There are lots of subconscious persuasive words that an individual may make use of. Frequently these will be a call to action: for instance, "Do that" or perhaps "Be this." Kind words as well as adjectives, for example, "Definitely," "Most," as well as "Effective," are extremely persuasive all on their very own.

Utilize "now" words, including "today" or perhaps "at the moment" frequently to subliminally recommend urgency.

- **Rhetorical Questions**

Allowing the individual to believe for themselves is extremely motivating and can, therefore, be incredibly persuasive. Ask questions that engage them, and they are instantly open. This will even enable you to know more about them. Frequently this will persuade them they're making the decision when in reality, you've just steered them to this particular persuasion.

- **Eye Contact**

It's highly crucial to produce a great rapport with the individual you're attempting to persuade. Without eye contact, this is practically impossible. With non-threatening and consistent eye contact, you can develop trust. Include a real smile, plus persuasion will get so much easier.

Be Persuasive by Connecting Emotionally, Not Rationally

Anybody of legislative issues will tell you - people simply don't answer judiciously. They respond depending on sentiments. To convince someone, you ought to associate with them inwardly. Aristotle decided the three central parts of each enticing contention:

Ethos: the believability, information, mastery, authority, and height of the individual endeavoring to convince.

Logos: the allure of rationale, reason, psychological reasoning, realities, and information.

Poignancy: the appeal to the feelings; the non-psychological, non-thinking inspirations affect activities just as decisions.

All layers are, obviously, vital. However, it's likely the mental Stage which keeps presumably the most energy of influence. We're mental creatures and are significantly more adept at being convinced by the guarantee of feeling extraordinary rather than the guarantee of "something being right."

The Moral Behind Persuasion Techniques

You may be reasoning that utilizing influence techniques is unethical, underhand. You may wind up with the problem of whether to use them on somebody you appreciate. In reality, it is up to you precisely how you consider utilizing viable techniques yet recall the accompanying. People must be aware of the systems and comprehend when others are endeavoring to control them. If you viably convince someone, you've recently out contended them.

Influence is discretionary. After training, that is definitely, and you may find that these compelling strategies are embedded into the elements. Might you feel regretful for utilizing different components of the uniqueness of yours, such as talking unquestionably? A ton of the time, you'll be endeavoring to do what's generally valuable for these individuals in any case. The objective of interfacing with somebody mentally is to realize what they need. At whatever point you understand this, you're simply convincing them to accomplish something which they will need to do in any case. Thus, by its meaning, influence isn't controlled - it's just bringing the purpose of yours over.

People must be satisfied to settle on their own decisions. In a perfect world, you should be certain to utilize these powerful strategies to do what's suitable for those concerned.

The intensity of Conscious Persuasion

The way into the universe is the strength of influence. Influence is the one key component to getting all you require, getting rich, and accomplishing whatever. With no influence, nothing completes. It's tied in with convincing yourself as well as other people. Influence is tied in with moving cognizance, and once you can move awareness, you can move something of the universe.

All influence is convincing to make a move, regardless of whether physical or mental exercise. Best and affluent people are experts of influence. You may have had specific ideas against utilizing influence since you feel it's controlled. In any case, they're restricting convictions that you have that are keeping you from accomplishment. The usage of influence for illegitimate reasons for existing controls. However, the normal utilization of influence is really for direction. Customers wish to be guided in a way that makes them agreeable and anxious to make a move to support themselves. We all need to be driven into doing what is superb for us by somebody who could show us the way.

Understanding that notion generates reality. Persuasion is all about changing the perception of individuals to change the reality theirs. It's about helping others to see things in a diverse way that they did not see before. To make use of persuasion, you initially need to persuade yourself about the usage of persuasion. You've to change the perception of yours of persuasion. If you can shift your beliefs and perception about truth to successful and wealthy people, you can utilize the strength of persuasion in the manner they put it to use.

Probably the most powerful as well as important individuals on the planet are the persuaders. They have the potential to shift people's perceptions, choices, and beliefs about things. If you would like to alter the planet, you've to alter the consciousness of individuals. The most effective persuasion is persuasion that moves individuals to the path they currently wish to go. It's persuasion to show them the ways of getting that which they wish. You can persuade men and women to do something if they believe it is going to satisfy them. In full persuasion, the objective is persuading individuals they have a particular desire, exactly how they can satisfy that motivation, and that it's worth whatever they provide in exchange for that that will meet the desire of theirs.

Numerous locations teach persuasion in different ways; however, the basic concepts all come right down to a couple of representing all of them. It's about getting attention and sparking curiosity and interest. In that case, it's related to arousing desire and convincing them to take a particular action to fulfill that desire. The crucial point that all persuasion deals with is convincing others about the importance of something. Something just has greatly based on the importance which you give it. Who's saying that a specific product is worth a specific amount of cash? The fact is that everything in the universe is free. All of the items in life obtain their worth from the perception of individuals. The perception of worth can differ from one individual to yet another. You can develop some worth in anything merely by the way you cause others to perceive it.

Nothing in the universe is actually of any use to any being except by the consciousness that the being has towards it. All drugs medications wouldn't do the job to heal whether an individual thinks that they wouldn't heal, and their consciousness isn't in harmony for healing but illness. For an individual with the consciousness and trust for healing, a placebo would procure the outcome of healing. Nobody can get pleasure from anything until they have the consciousness to get satisfaction from that thing.

It's persuasion that makes the world go round. When individuals aren't persuaded to do anything, there'd be no movement of energy. There'd be no buying or even selling. When materials aren't being moved around, things can't be placed into the hands of those who could place them to use more effectively. The economy comes to a standstill when cash isn't flowing. When individuals keep what they've rather than offer to get something far more, it'll just lead to stagnation, entropy, and the universe's degrading.

That's why the entrepreneurs and sales promoters are doing society a huge service. By convincing individuals to see value in food and offer something different, whether it's time, information, or money to get it, they're encouraging power exchange. When power is replaced, that's when there could be experienced types and brand-new combinations of energy designed for the majority around the globe to benefit from. The exchange of electrical power is the thing that supports the evolution of humanity and also the improvement of living.

PART 2

Chapter 14: What Is Dark Psychology?

Dark Psychology involves the study of the human experience as it refers to individuals' psychological nature of preying on other individuals motivated by unlawful and/or deviant intentions that lack meaning and particular assumptions of instinctual motives and the concept of social science. All human civilization has the potential to harm other human beings and living things. Although this ability is restrained or sublimated by many, a few other activities on such urges.

Dark Psychology attempts to understand such thoughts, emotions, perceptions, and structures of subjective handling that give rise to predatory behaviors that are directly opposed to contemporary human behavioral understandings. Dark Psychology implies that unlawful, deviant, and violent characteristics are intentional, and 99.99 percent of the time do have reasonable goal-oriented ambition. It is the remaining parts.01 percent, Dark Psychology from Adlerian theory and Teleology. There is an area within the human mind that Dark Psychology postulates enables some individuals to carry atrocious acts without intent.

Dark Psychology asserts that all mankind has a reserve of malevolent purpose against others varying from minimally intrusive and transient thinking to absolute psychopathic deviant actions lacking some coherent reason. It is named the Dark Continuum. Mitigating factors that act as accelerators and/or attractants to encounter the Dark Singularity, and where horrific actions of a person fall upon the Dark Continuum, is what Dark Psychology calls Dark element. Dark Psychology is a notion that I have been grappling with for 15 years. It was only recently that I finally formulated the meaning, psychology, and philosophy of this human experience aspect.

Dark Psychology includes everything that helps make us who we are related to our evil side. This proverbial cancer is present in all societies, all faiths, and all of human existence. From the time we are born to the moment of death, within us there is an aspect of wandering that some have named immoral and others have categorized as unlawful, deviant, and psychopathic. Dark Psychology brings a third philosophical concept which gives a different view to these behaviors as compared to religious dogmas and ideas of modern social science.

Some individuals commit these same actions in Dark Psychology and do so for power, money, romantic love, vengeance, or any other recognized intent. Without a target, they commit those horrendous acts. In simple words, its ends don't justify its means. There are individuals who for the sake of doing so defy and wound others. That potential lies within each of us. The area which I explore is the possibility to harm someone without cause, justification, or intent. Dark Psychology implies that this dark potentiality is extremely complicated and even harder to describe.

Dark Psychology implies that we all have the ability for predator behaviors, and this capability has the full right to our thoughts, feelings, and experiences. We all have this capability as you will learn throughout this book, but only some of us act upon them. At one time or another, we all had feelings and thoughts about intending to behave painfully. We have all had thoughts that we want to seriously damage others without kindness. If you're truthful with yourself, you'll have to agree that you've had ideas and feel like you want to do heinous deeds.

Because of the fact, we perceive ourselves to be some kind of virtuous species; one would want to assume that these feelings and thoughts would not emerge. Sadly, all of us have these ideas, and thankfully, never practice them. Dark Psychology suggests that there are individuals who have similar ideas, emotions, and experiences but operate upon them in a meticulously planned or impulsive fashion. The important distinction is that they respond to them whereas others have merely short-lived thoughts and emotions to do so.

Dark Psychology claims that this type of predator is intentional and has a certain logical, purpose-oriented motive. Religious belief, philosophy, psychology, and other belief systems have been cogent in their ways to explain Dark Psychology. It is true that almost all human behavior, connected to evil actions, is purposeful and purpose-oriented, though

Dark Psychology implies that there is a region where purposeful behavior and purpose-oriented motivation appear to become vague. There is a spectrum of maltreatment of Dark Psychology varying from opinions to pure deranged deviance, with no evident reasoning or purpose. This spectrum, Dark Continuum, allows the Dark Psychology philosophy to be conceived.

Dark Psychology identifies that aspect of the human psyche or basic human status that enables unethical behavior and can even help persuade it. Some of the features of this behavior change are the absence of apparently reasonable motivation, its universality as well as its lack of clarity in many instances. This basic human condition is assumed by Dark Psychology to be different or an outgrowth of evolution. Let's dig at those very simple evolutionary tenets. First, consider that we evolved from many other animals and are the shining beacon of all animal life at present. Our frontal lobe enabled us to become the entity at the peak. Now let us presume that being alpha predators doesn't exempt us from our animal impulses and aggressive behavior.

How Dark Psychology Works?

The more guests can envision Dark Psychology, the much better set up they wind up to diminish their exploitation opportunities by human hunters. Before continuing, it is basic to have, at any rate, a little cognizance of Dark Psychology. As you continue through future original copies widening this build, this creator will clarify concerning one of the fundamental standards. Coming up next are six principles important to acknowledge Dark Psychology as clings to: at last.

1. Dark Psychology is a worldwide piece of the human condition. This development has had an impact from the beginning of time. All social orders, social orders, and people that dwell in them keep this feature of human wellbeing. The most generous people comprehended have this evil domain, yet never follow up on it and have lower paces of savage thoughts and sensations.

2. It is the investigation of the human condition as it identifies with people's musings, sentiments, and suppositions associated with this intrinsic potential to go after others without obvious, distinct reasons. Thought about that all conduct is purposive, objective arranged, and conceptualized utilizing business, as usual, Dark Psychology advances the thought the closer an individual pulls in to the "dark opening" of excellent mischievousness, the less in all likelihood he/she has a reason in motivations. Even though this essayist assumes lovely evil is never gotten to, Dark Psychology thinks some approach because it is boundless.

3. Because of its chance of error as unusual psychopathy, Dark Psychology might be disregarded in its unexposed structure. The foundation is stacked with cases of this unexposed affinity to unveil itself as dynamic, hurtful propensities. Present-day psychiatry and brain research characterizes the crazy as a hunter lacking regret for his exercises. Dim Psychology says a continuum of power goes from considerations just as vibes of actual brutality to outrageous exploitation and actual maltreatment without a viable goal or motivation.

4. In this congruity, the Dark Psychology's seriousness isn't viewed as less or significantly more horrifying by exploitation activities, anyway stories out an assortment of savagery. A direct picture would be differentiating Ted Bundy and Jeffrey Dahmer. Both were extreme psychos, just as loathsome in their activities. The thing that matters has Dahmer dedicated his godawful homicides for his silly interest in kinship while Ted Bundy killed, and cruelly brought upon distress out of incredible hysterical mischievousness. Both would be more noteworthy on the Dark Continuum, yet one, Jeffrey Dahmer, can be better perceived utilizing his sad maniacal necessity to be delighted in.

5. Dark Psychology thinks all individuals have the potential for actual brutality. This potential is natural in all individuals, and diverse inside, just as external factors raise the likelihood of appearing ok into temperamental propensities. These propensities are ruthless, just as now and again; they can work without factor. Dull Psychology accepts the hunter prey dynamic becomes deformed by individuals. Dull Psychology is a human sensation and shared by nothing else than a living creature. True savagery and even turmoil may exist in different other living life forms, yet humanity is the main assortment that can do so without reason.

6. A comprehension of the fundamental reasons and triggers of Dark Psychology would better permit the way of life to perceive, distinguish just as maybe decrease the threats naturally in its impact. Finding the thoughts of Dark Psychology serves as a twofold helpful component. At first, tolerating most of us having these opportunities for evil permits

those with this aptitude to diminish their likelihood of emitting. Second of all, grasping the fundamentals of Dark Psychology accommodates our unique, extraordinary goal for battling to endure.

This present's creator will likely illuminate others by upgrading their mindfulness, building up a standard to improve their fact, and persuading them to advise others to attempt to discover to limit the chance of capitulating to those had by the weights investigated by it. If you have been a casualty or prey of the guided executioner, don't feel mortified since we as a whole encounter some sort of exploitation at some time in our lives.

The majority of us have a dark side. It turns out to be important for the human condition, be that as it may, made a deal to avoid being all around perceived. An unwanted reality, Dark Psychology, fringes us standing by quietly to strike. As this creator has once in the past expressed, Dark Psychology incorporates a wide range of horrible and fierce propensities. We need to take a gander at the careless savagery of pets. Being a dedicated family pet fan, pet abuse to this author is both brutal and psychopathic. As late examinations have proposed, creature abuse partners with a higher likelihood of giving brutality against humankind.

On the milder side of the Dark brain, science is a defacement of other private property or the expanding levels of savagery in computer games youths, just as youngsters, advocate during the occasion. Pulverization just as a kid's interest to play horrendous PC games are gently differentiated to unmistakable brutality yet are express instances of this worldwide human property this present creator's idea features. By far, most of humanity denies just as conceals its reality, yet still, the parts of Dark Psychology quietly stow away underneath the surface in all individuals.

It is general and wherever all through society. Some strict convictions indicate it as a natural element they call Satan. A few societies depend on the presence of underhanded powers, just like the miscreants causing malignant exercises. A few societies' most splendid have characterized Dark Psychology as a mental condition or brought forth by hereditary characteristics passed down from age to age.

This author examines Dark Psychology's origin and nature to understand how the standard, a well-socialized individual can wind up current, having dedicated a wrong no one can have forecasted. During the day and throughout the evening, wrongs caused by one human on one more occur because of the beginning of recorded history. Although horrible, it is incredible how decent people can perhaps participate in or enable such horrors to occur.

Thousands of these wrongs appear throughout the background. The holocaust throughout The second world war, as well as ethnic cleansing currently taking place in neighboring nations, are a few instances. Experience, with the residues of what Dark Psychology has caused, is plentiful with cases. As explained above, Dark Psychology is alive and well and also requires a close examination. As you continue to discover the tenets and foundation of Dark Psychology, a cognitive structure of understanding will slowly establish.

Understanding Dark Persuasion

The first difference you will notice between positive and dark persuasion is the motive behind it. Positive persuasion is used to encourage someone to complete an action that will cause them any harm. In some cases, such as with the negotiator saving a hostage, this persuasion can help save lives.

But with dark persuasion, there isn't any form of a moral motive. The motive is usually amoral and often immoral. If positive persuasion is understood to help people help themselves, then dark persuasion makes people act against their self-interest. Sometimes, people will do these actions begrudgingly, knowing that they are probably not making the right choice, but they do it because they are eager to stop the ongoing persuasion efforts. In other cases, the best dark persuader will make their victim think that they acted wisely, but the victim is doing the opposite in that case.

So, what are the motivations for someone who is a dark persuader? This is going to depend on the situation and the individual who is doing the persuading. Some people like to persuade their victims to serve their self-interests. Others are going to act through with the intention just to cause some harm to the other person. In some cases, the persuader will not benefit from darkly persuading their victim, but they do so because they want to inflict pain on the other person. And still, others enjoy the control that this kind of persuasion gives to them.

You will also find that the outcome you get from dark persuasion will differ from positive persuasion. With positive persuasion, you are going to get one of three scenarios, including the following:

- The benefit goes to the person who is being persuaded.
- There is a win/win benefit for the persuaded and the persuader.
- There is a mutual benefit for the person who is persuaded and a third party.

These outcomes are good because they will involve a positive result for the person who is being persuaded. Sometimes, there will be others who benefit from these actions. But out of all three situations, the persuaded party is always going to benefit.

With dark persuasion, the outcome is going to be very different. The persuader is the one who will always benefit when they exercise their need for influence or control. The one who is being persuaded often goes against what is in their self-interest when they listen, and they are not going to benefit from all this dark persuasion.

Besides, the most skilled dark persuaders cannot only cause some harm to their victims while also benefiting themselves, but they could also end up harming others in the process.

Unmasking the Dark Persuader

At this point, you may be curious about who is using these dark methods of persuasion. Are there people out there who are interested in using this kind of persuasion and using it against others to cause harm?

A dark persuader's main characteristics are either an indifference toward or an inability to care about how persuasion will impact others. Such people who use this kind of persuasion are often selfish and will see their own needs as more important than others' needs. They may even be sociopathic and unable to grasp the idea of someone else's emotions.

Many times, this kind of dark persuasion is going to show up in a relationship. Often, both partners are going to be inclined to use dark persuasion on each other. If these attempts are persistent and endure, then this type of relationship will be classified as psychologically abusive, and that is not healthy for the victim in that relationship. They will often not realize that something is going on or are darkly persuaded until it is too late, and they are stuck there.

There are many examples of using this kind of dark persuasion in a relationship. If one partner stops the other partner from taking a new job opportunity or doesn't allow them to go out with friends, this could be an example of dark persuasion. The dark persuader will convince the victim that they are acting in the best way for the relationship. In reality, the victim is going through a process that harms them and the relationship.

Chapter 15: Indoctrination Strategies

As you read familiar words, be aware of what they intend and disguise. Uncover this content in front of you and others. Before you take words in essential matters, check to see if those words fit your goals. Words can prevent or facilitate proper knowledge of the problem.

Do not recklessly accept other people's words but try to express your ideas in your own words. Do not take on the problems or the alternatives of your opponents but formulate yourself the problem or the alternatives. Check what and with which words are you regularly sprinkled or indoctrinated. Which messages do you always hear, who is trying to keep your attention in constant control? To what extent have you already come to terms with someone else's ideas? For example, did you notice that in the spring of 2007, a car manufacturer rented 80 percent of all billboards in Germany and Switzerland for several weeks to publicize a new car model? Maybe even three years following, you can remember which model that was.

Make a regular game of scrutinizing the advertising that you encounter critically for their actual information content. Distinguish between information and sentiment. Also, think about which external influences you can entirely or partially escape. Autonomy means self-determination and, as a prerequisite, also requires distance, rest, and time with oneself.

Often advertising with popular spots is targeted at children. When they then lurk advertisements all day long, they become tools of subtle indoctrination. This is particularly effective in making it even harder for children to turn off than watching TV.

The fact that in most private broadcasters, the most exciting films are interrupted abruptly, especially in the most dramatic moments by a suddenly breaking advertising message, is not only a disgrace for the spectator, but also aims at the very moments in which one with the largest internal openness sits in front of the screen. You can protect yourself and your children against such psychoterrorism by providing targeted broadcasters without advertising or DVDs.

In his article The One-Dimensional Man, social philosopher Herbert Marcuse wrote that people in modern society had lost sight of alternatives. You would usually only see and recognize one side of things. This is the one associated with the familiar or dominant word creations.

This process is a prerequisite for opinion dictatorship, for one-sidedness and lack of tolerance. In order not to become so one-dimensional yourself, you should always strive for alternative thinking. Everyone knows that everything has two sides, but who lives by that principle? Open accordingly for counter positions or views that are foreign to you or that you would reject. If you try to get involved, you will most likely discover meaningful aspects of the truth in it.

Try to break out of conventional thinking and to think differently about situations or situations. Develop alternative problem solving or life designs. Imagine a few castles in the air or plan your election campaign and design a concept of your world politics. Think about what might be wrong in the right direction and what could be recommended in the forbidden.

Think across! At least mentally break out of your usual horizons again and again. Our company, your company, you are good at alternatives, goals, dreams, and visions. They are the sources of new and meaningful developments.

To find out what has influenced you so much, you should, with some distance, once again clarify the persons, circumstances, milieus, scenes, and groups you coined, as well as the family, the party, and Worldview in which you grew up. If you wonder which motive and interest you have been doing so manipulated in, you may be able to think of clearing out some of them more clearly and working out your own identity and your own will.

You may also wonder how your preferences match those of the groups you currently belong to. The greater the correspondence you see in detail, the more likely you assume that your thinking is foreign. Then think about the points you differ from the group opinion and try to communicate that as well. The resistance you encounter will make you realize how convinced the group is.

In principle, you should also consult and weigh up other opinions and positions before making your own opinion on an important issue.

The so-called climatic catastrophe does not seem to threaten as much as it has been propagated in the media over a longer period. It would be better to a possible Climate change, and its currently still unpredictable consequences of speaking.

If you find yourself constantly in agreement with many other people's opinions, you should become restless. Maybe you are over-adjusted. In many cases, education amounts to making one flexible and adaptable. The less one's own identity is formed, the less opinionated and stubborn one becomes, the easier it is to follow instructions and commands. Children were brought up to follow. If this becomes a life principle beyond puberty, the pedagogically desirable goal of maturing is not achieved. Being mature means having your own opinion and being able to say it.

Trust your judgment more than anyone else. Have the courage to express your opinion even where you have to expect contradictions and do it wisely and kindly.

How Can You Influence Others?

How far you can influence the consciousness of groups or society depends, in part, on your position and the attentiveness to that position. The more public attention you have, the further your impact will be.

Influences can also be created artificially. Groups, businesses, individuals are doing public relations to get known. This is trying to attract attention. If that does not succeed in the positive, then if necessary, also in the negative. The main thing is to get attention, get in the public perception, and remain in the conversation. Methods to gain attention are:

- Leaving the conventions
- Breaking the rules of normalcy
- Do something extraordinary
- Violated expectations
- Do something crazy
- Provoke by taboos
- Making noise and causing a stir

You can build a positive image by associating yourself or your name with perceptions, feelings, objects, or attitudes that create positive emotions in other people. Also, by strengthening others' self-esteem through recognition, praise, or compliments, you can elicit positive feelings from them. These are most likely to be returned to you.

Once you have ranked high, anything you say following will have a higher recognition value. Your confirmation will make you appear as a well-meaning ally whose expertise will not be called into question for a moment. Depending on how you need it, you can add a positive or negative color to your words. One way of upgrading is to substitute one word for another, positive one:

- Preserved thickened milk mucus from the can for the Coffee is sold as a lucky clover.

- A journal becomes the essence of the latest findings.

- A health insurance company becomes a health insurance fund.

- It is not a pair of jeans which are sold, but a sexy butt.

- Another way to add value is to add a positive adjective or epithet to nouns:

- Lunch becomes a delicious meal or a culinary delight.

- Politics becomes a forward-looking peace policy.

- A written report becomes a comprehensive report or - with the substitution of the noun - a concise conclusion.

- A birthday party becomes a funny birthday party or even a special event for a friend.

In the devaluation, one proceeds analogously and plot terms negatively:

- From the delicious birthday cake, it becomes one fat calorie bomb.
- The five-star hotel becomes a bonze shed.
- The luxury sedan becomes a pimp sleigh.
- The street musician becomes a noisy beggar.

In this way, you can try to make things appear in the light you want to show them. It greatly increases the likelihood that your message will arrive as you wish.

Enemy images are negative ways of identifying oneself from which one delimits oneself. Whoever declares anyone or anything to be the cause of all evil and at the same time conveys to the addressee the feeling that they have nothing in common with this cause of all evil can easily expose himself as the savior from ruin and pull the people to his side:

Firstly, if the Taliban and Al Qaeda are evil and try to expand, you can consider yourself good because you are not one or the other. Secondly, you must become active to do something about evil. After all, one cannot allow his expansion to be inactive. If someone tells you what to do about it, you can hardly say anything against it. They would eventually recognize themselves as sympathizers of the wicked.

A Chancellor is often called a Chancellor of the Peace. This name does not miss its effect. He also assumes that a possible counter-candidate is not a peace chancellor by claiming this title for himself. Simple models are the easiest to implement; they do not require thinking. Therefore, it is effective to reduce complicated issues to simple formulas.

The slogan " War on Terrorism " probably drew so much because most citizens used the term " terrorism." Thus, the war is finally as undesirable. Still, necessary minor evil in the fight against the larger accepted and considered justified.

Keywords should be so simple and clear that they remain present in every consciousness and activate a reasonably clear association field:

- The slightly different restaurant
- China in the Olympic fever
- Juppies (young urban professional people)
- Dinks (double income, no kids)
- Generation Golf

Appealing to and building on similarities makes it easier for you to be heard and, on that basis, to continue to pursue your true concern. So, you can pick up people at a joint meeting point and take them to your destination.

Constant repetition makes the alleged confidant more familiar and, therefore, more credible. This applies to the propaganda for wars in the present just as it did in antiquity: The older one, Cato, is said to have been in the Roman Senate for several years. Every one of his speeches begins with the phrase: By the way, I favor the motion that Carthage must be destroyed. He reached his goal indeed: It came to the Third Punic War, and Carthage was destroyed.

A question mark is like a hook on which something always gets stuck! Questions are apt to dispel suspicions and rumors:

- Is Mr. X cheating on his wife? Or

- Minister Y transferred the embezzlement of taxpayers' money?

- Why does Uncle deny abuse of his niece?

The language includes a rich and ingenious repertoire of possibilities to achieve and to move considerably. Depending on the intentions and interests of a speaker, this can result in great dangers, including people's disempowerment and the initiation of wars. In the service of a selfish and power-hungry manipulator, the power and magic of language can become a curse.

On the other hand, whoever wants to serve a good cause will be less successful if he tries naively to speak as his beak has grown for him. He can only effectively fulfill his request if he has as many registers in his language as possible and knows how to use them virtuoso.

Chapter 16: Brainwashing

Brainwashing is a tactic that we often hear. We are told that television commercials bombard us with what to buy, and we are exposed to people's rants on television, radio, the newspaper, online, and social media. These rants tell us what we should look like, what we should be eating, reading, voting for, wearing, etc. We are all subjected to the art of brainwashing daily, and the amount of brainwashing continues to grow.

Before the creation of social media, we were still exposed to social media. However, they would only market to their target audience. If they weren't meant for you, they would be ignored until the after commercial or show came back on the air. For example, you wouldn't have paid much attention to a Polly Pocket or Barbie commercial unless you were a ten-year-old girl or someone who might buy the product for their child.

But things are not like that anymore. Advertising has moved past gender roles, and with the inception of social media, advertisements are now personally geared for us. These websites take information that we provide them. For instance, Facebook uses our likes, comments, status updates, etc., to find the perfect things to advertise. They are utilizing brainwashing techniques in the 21st century.

Today, we are bombarded with mind control techniques daily. There are many different types and levels of mind control. We will go over an overview of the types, and we'll talk about some examples of them. There are three basic levels of mind control. Each level corresponds with a different type of psychology. So far, no technology can control what you choose to believe. So we will talk about the methods to defend it, and we will also look at some of the implications it has on civilizations. Mind control skills are used wrong for obvious reasons, whether it's politically or scientifically speaking. Simply by existing in a society, we are constantly subject to manipulation or indoctrination.

The first-level appeals to consciousness. The second level corresponds to unconsciousness, and the last level appeals to biological. Now in terms of psychology, the first one, consciousness, has to do with cognitive psychology. Cognitive means being aware of what's going on. The second one is unconsciousness, which corresponds with behavioral psychology and while the last one is biological psychology, which talks about psychiatry. This is where you can try to control the mind using physical things like drugs and electrical shock. Every mind control technique fits into its methods. Some of the mind-control techniques will fit into one of these levels, while some mind techniques will fit in between two of them. But every mind control technique fits inside the sun part of the chart. Now let us talk about the different levels of my control and what fits in between.

The Conscious Level

The first level is the conscious level. This level is the level that deals with information. It does not talk about punishment or physical pain. It appeals to your reason. The basic forms of this are education and ideological indoctrination.

A good example of this is when you get your driver's license. You decide to take fighting classes, and you learn the rules of the road, and the intention is to make you behave a certain way when you are driving. Now, most people don't have a problem with this because if you don't behave a certain way when you drive, you will have a problem.

So ideological indoctrination is the worldview and philosophy, and what you're educated in, in your worldview. So, this includes your political choice, education, religious education, and even your science education. Now this means how do you view the world and by what you were dictated by. Now, at this level, you have to mention the fact, which means information. Now because propaganda has been abused in the past, people normally have a negative view of it.

Now the basic idea is that somebody wants you to view the world differently, so they educate you. Propaganda is just information control. Now information control isn't that bad. For instance, have you ever seen a billboard that says that 50000 people die when driving and drinking? Now that is propaganda, and it is not bad. Hitler used propaganda to educate Germany into the idea that all Germany's problem was because of the Jews. Now that is bad propaganda.

The Unconscious or Behavioral Psychology

Now let's look at the after level of mind control, which is unconscious or behavioral psychology. This does not appeal to the Conscious mind. It is an attempt to control somebody without his or her conscious decision being involved. The biggest school of psychology is behavioral psychology that comes from Pablo psychology. A great example of that is the story of the man who rings the bell for the dog to salivate that we talked about above. So this deals with stimulus-response. Stimulus means when something happens – in the man and the dog case, it's ringing the bell. Response - in the man and the dog case, is the dog's drooling. Now, this does not appear to be a conscious mind. The dog did not decide to salivate; they just did it automatically. Now, unlike the Conscious level, this level often includes physical pain, punishment, and torment.

For instance, you can implant a commanding chip in somebody so that when they hear the command, which is the stimulus, they will go and do something, which is the response. It is a stimulus-response. The person that is programmed to do that thing doesn't decide to do it because it is an automatic response, and in fact, he doesn't even know that he is being programmed because that thing is in the subconscious. At this point, we have hypnosis, and the reason it's so is that hypnosis is implanted into the subconscious.

For instance, the operator says: when I say bubble gum, bark like a dog. So, the stimulus is the bubblegum, whereas the response is the barking like a dog. Or the operator says: when I snap my fingers, you should act like a stripper. So, he snaps his fingers, which is the stimulus, and acting like a stripper is the response. Creating a stimulus-response mechanism is called conditioning. Part of the conditioning is programming somebody to associate pain or pleasure with something. Now another part of this level is called punishment. Punishment is an attempt to make somebody associate pain with undesirable behavior.

Now let's go with: if you have a kid and the kid flicks the switch off. Now on the Conscious level, you could sit your child down and explain why it is wrong, and hopefully, your child would decide not to do it again. Now on the unconscious level, you can beat the hell out of the child until the child tends to associate pain with switching the switch off and hope and hope that doesn't do it again.

Behaviorism attempts to control somebody's behavior, like how you train a dog using rewards and punishments. Now the cognitive approach is the best, and this is the level where we have brainwashing or interrogation. And you will do this using physical pain to control someone. Another note about brainwashing is that it has the word washing, which means wipe something away and wash it away. The word brainwashing comes from a technique that was used in China, which is called political re-education. The idea is that when you want to wash something away, you put something else in its place.

In the MK-ultra program, the psychiatrist called it de-patterning. Now when you take somebody from their religion and use mind control techniques, you will be able to wipe out their religious beliefs and put another belief in his place. This is called programming. So under brainwashing, we have political re-education, we have the patterning, and we also have religious education or de-programming.

Biological Psychology

Now the last level is Biology, which equates to biological psychology or psychiatrist. Now at this level, you are attempting to control someone's behavior through physical interventions. Physical interventions include brain surgery, drugs, electrical shock, or implanting something into the brain. Now for the child who flipped the switch off, the cognitive approach will be sitting the child down and explaining why it is wrong now. The behavioral approach will be to spank him, and the biological approach will be to give him a psychotic drug. Or a remote-control robot. Now those are the basic levels. Many different mind control techniques fit into these levels, but we will not be going deep into them.

There are different levels to control somebody's behavior between the Conscious and unconscious levels, and we are constantly subjected to this daily. One of these techniques is public relations, and it is aimed to make you feel a certain way about something. Now, this is not to just make you feel good about something. It can make you feel bad about a competitor, a group, or a person. And it is called Black public relations. Now another mind control technique is marketing and advertising. Another mind control technique that falls between the Conscious and unconscious level of mind control is pandering, and the word pandering means to fulfill a moral desire, a prostitute pandering to a sexual desire, a drug dealer pandering to an addiction.

So, what this means is that you're controlling someone by giving them what they want. Under pandering, future control by destruction is included, including television, pornography, and video games. And another mind-control technique on the biological level is addiction. Manipulative people keep their victims to them by making them addicted to drugs. And beyond that, there is a reason why caffeine has been added to soft drinks, and there is a reason why energy has been added to fast food, and there is a reason why sugar is added to almost everything in the grocery store; it's because it is a type of mind control.

Now the last technique, which is at the very bottom, is when you give up on trying to control the person's mind and restrain them. An example is a straightjacket, institutionalization, imprisonment, and heavy tranquilizer. If everything fails and you can't control the person's mind, there is still something left to shoot the person. So that is basically what dark psychology brainwashing is all about.

Chapter 17: Body Language

Body language encompasses the gestures and motions we can interpret to make sense of someone else's emotions or feelings. These cues consist of posture, gestures, facial expressions, use of space, and touch. Both human beings and animals use body language to communicate, though early human beings relied more heavily on this communication form than modern man.

Nobody is sure whether we are born with the ability to read body language or acquire the ability to grow up. However, most people are capable—at least at some level—of reading and interpreting body language. The reason why nobody is sure how we acquire this ability is two-fold. Firstly, body language can be divided into numerous categories.

Understanding what my behavior display

Some people are natural at reading others, but they couldn't tell you how they know what they know. That's because they are intuitively reading others' body language, but they don't have the knowledge to define why they are such good communicators. More than 70 percent of the messages we send and receive are through nonverbal language. Not only are the greatest percent of our messages nonverbal, but that nonverbal language is more honest and genuine than the words we speak. Our bodies don't sugarcoat the message; we just respond and react without being conscious of doing so.

If people are saying one thing but their body language is delivering a different message, put more stock in what you see than what you hear. However, to make sure you are reading the person correctly, let's discuss all the different nonverbal messages we send. We'll cover the nonverbal signals and what they might mean, but keep in mind that different cultures and countries might attach a different meaning to your body language. When you're confused about the nonverbal message that another is sending, then listen to the words and take the signals in context with the phrases they use.

Another way to determine the message is through the tone, pitch, and volume of another's voice. It gives truth to that saying, "It's not what you said but how you said it." When all these things are examined during your analysis of others, you'll find clarity in the message. While we're at it, there is one more thing—pay attention to the other person's required personal space. If you are questioning whether the message they are sending is positive, negative, or benevolent, step inside their personal space and be aware of their reaction. Their feelings will then be quite pronounced. If the message was meant to be off-putting, they will immediately step back or adopt a space-claiming stance that will let you know their feelings in no uncertain terms.

Facial Expressions, Features, and Head Movement

Playing with Hair and Moving the Head

If someone slides their fingers through their hair at the temples and tosses their head back, this is an indication they might be flirting with you. On the other hand, if they are running their fingers through their hair from their forehead through the top of their crown, that is a sign they are confused or frustrated. Tilting the head and twirling the hair is also a flirtatious mannerism, indicating interest combined with a little nervous tension.

When people nod their heads, it matters how many times they do so before stopping. For example, public speakers who are attentive to their audiences know that three nods mean interest and attentiveness. However, if you observe a group of people conversing, you'll notice the person who nods their head only once is eager to leave and will probably be the next one to make a quick exit.

If someone is interested in what you're saying, they will often tilt their head in your direction. They could be showing curiosity or questioning what you are saying when they bring one ear closer to make sure they are getting every detail of the conversation.

Eye Movement

People usually blink six or seven times a minute, but those who are stressed blink quite a bit more. If someone covers their eyes with their hands, excessively rubs their eyes, or closes their eyes, they could be hiding something or feel threatened. When the eyes are shifty or rapidly moving from one person to another, it reflects some scattered thoughts that are going on in their heads. If there is a flickering interest between two people when this is happening, then it can also be a way for people to prevent detection as they were checking out the other.

If someone has a habit of not making eye contact or looking down as they speak, it can show shyness or can also be a cry for empathy. They are waiting for you to ask what's wrong and open the way for them to share their feelings. Investigators have come to realize that a sustained glance from a person who denies involvement in a crime, may mean they are lying and trying to overcompensate by looking them straight in the eyes for a long time to show they're telling the truth.

If you have posted a question and the person you asked looks upward, they are most likely trying to picture something they saw. On the other hand, if they look to the side toward their ear, they could be trying to recall a message they heard. If they look downward after your question, they are connecting your question with something negative and trying to find a way to avoid answering or revealing their feelings about the matter.

Eyebrow Movement

If individuals raise their eyebrows, it usually means the person is curious about or interested in your conversation. A quick popup of one eyebrow could be a flirtation, and if the eyebrow is raised a bit longer, it often means that the other person doesn't quite buy into what you say.

If the brows furrow, you can almost bet that person is having second thoughts about what is being done or said. It most likely indicates a negative emotion like fear or confusion, so it might be time for you to back off a bit.

Lips

Of course, a smile sends a universal message, if it is truly a smile. We've all been at the other end of a fake smile, which is one that doesn't travel to the eyes and makes them wrinkle in agreement. We call those "Red Carpet" smiles. They are Hollywood smiles given by people who are trying to be friendly to their fans but just want to get inside, sit down, and make it through the night.

Individuals who plaster a smile on their face almost all the time, are usually nervous. If it's in the workplace, they could feel out-of-their-depth or incompetent. There's a good chance that foreigners who smile a lot don't understand a blasted thing, so they just smile and nod.

Another thing people do with their lips is to suck on them and bite them. Sucking or biting the lip is a reaction by those who need to settle themselves down. Like a newborn, the action soothes them and offers a bit of comfort in a stressful situation. If one clamps down on their lips or purses them, it can mean frustration or anger.

Body and Limb Movements

Body Positions

If there is a group of people standing and talking and one or more people open their bodies to you, that is an invitation to join the conversation. If they just turn their head, you might want to choose another group. You will know if you have captured the attention of a love interest because he or she will turn slightly toward you and point their feet in your direction, to indicate they are interested in finding out what makes you tick. If you step into the group and the person beside you touches your shoulder or arm, this is a direct ploy to show you they are interested in exploring the relationship a bit further.

When you step into the group, if the person beside you leans in to you, they genuinely like you. If their head retracts backward, perhaps something you said surprised or offended them. If they physically lean away from you, they've already made up their mind that they're not going to listen to or like you. If they turn their head in the opposite direction and follow it with their shoulder, you just got the cold shoulder. So, forget about it!

Standing Positions

If someone is standing with legs about shoulder-width apart, it often is a sign of dominance and determination, as if they needed to stand their ground against something or prove a point. If they stand with legs together, front forward, they will hear you out, but you need to make your point quickly. When the person you are speaking with is standing and shifting their weight from side-to-side or front-to-back, it might indicate several things. They could be bored, or they are anxious and need to soothe themselves with this rocking sort of movement. To determine their feelings, it is necessary to look further at what they are doing with their arms as well.

Arm Positions

Don't assume that crossed arms always mean that the other person is upset. Not so! Some people will stand or sit with their arms crossed because it is just a comfortable position. You can distinguish the other's emotions by looking further at their facial expression. If they have furrowed eyebrows, their mouth pursed, and their arms crossed, chances are they are angry or upset about something. Crossed arms can also be a sign of protection or a closed attitude to the ideas you are presenting.

If someone is talking with their arms flopping around, it can mean they are excited and agreeable, or it can say that they are out of control. Again, you'll need to couple your observations with other nonverbal messages to be sure. Typically, people who are overly animated are less believable and have less control over their emotions, as well as having a lack of power. They flail their arms to gain attention as if to say "I'm talking now, so would somebody please listen to me?"

Leg and Foot Positions

People whose toes turn inward could be closing themselves off to your comments, or they could just be pigeon-toed. To determine if there is a physiological issue that causes their toes to point it, you might need more background information. Don't rush to judgment, just wait, observe more body language, and listen to their words. Some people who began turning in their toes because they were insecure or awkward, might have created a habit that they find difficult to break. The only message they are sending is one that says; I have a physical issue that is impacting my body language.

Sitting Positions

If a person is spread out all over your couch, they have a feeling of self-importance. On the other hand, they probably have a good deal of confidence as well. Legs open, leaning forward with elbows on knees shows an in-charge attitude that is still open to hearing what you have to say.

If a person is sitting next to you and crosses their legs at the knee, pointing their foot toward you, they are permitting you to approach them. If, however, they are sitting next to you and angle their body in the opposite direction, you're probably not going to engage or connect with him or her. If that same person is fidgeting, quickly moving their ankle or foot, they are looking for a way out. Excuse yourself; both of you will probably feel more comfortable.

Hands

When people sit on their hands, and the temperatures aren't below freezing, it could be an indication that they are deceitful trying to hide something from you. If they walk with their hands in their pockets or behind their back, they might be relaying information, but you're not getting the full picture because they are withholding information. When you look at one's fingers and see bitten nails or chewed cuticles, you can bet that it is a nervous person with low self-esteem. Or else they have put themselves in a situation that they find extremely uncomfortable.

When someone holds their hands like a church steeple and presses them to their lips, they have something important to add to the conversation but are trying to decide how to present their information. They are self-assured and will contribute when the time is right. These are the thinkers, the analytical types.

If the person is rubbing their legs with open palms pressed down, they are feeling vulnerable or uncomfortable with your nearness or your conversation. If nothing is said, don't think you are not sending a message that is perhaps louder than any words. Examine your body language and see what message you are sending to them that could be creating this reaction.

Walking

People who advance with rather large strides are purposeful and perceived as important and competent. People think those who walk with a little bounce in their step most likely have a positive nature. And those who walk hunched over with shoulders down—well, that kind of speaks for itself, doesn't it? They are probably prone to depression and wrapped a bit too tight.

What Does One's Voice Say About Them?

There are four indicators of the quality of one's voice. They are one's intonation, volume, pitch, and rate of speech. If the voice is monotone and rather flat, they are probably bored or boring. The lack of animation in the voice could also indicate the speaker is tired. If the person's voice sounds clear and concise, they most usually are confident and powerful, more like the Leader Personality Type. If the volume is quiet or soft, the person is thought to be shy, or it could even mean they have a secret they don't want to share.

The rate of speech is also quite important when analyzing others, especially if you are attempting to mirror them to increase the chances of connectivity. For example, Leader Personality Types will usually speak fast and loudly, and you need to match their volume and rate. Identifiers often speak slower than Leaders, and their pitch is more soothing than the dominant personality type. The voice can be a strong descriptive element of the individual's personality type.

By now, you have probably caught on that every movement has a message. Verify the meaning of some of the nonverbal languages by other things, such as one's words, voice, facial expressions, and gestures. To discover one's real message, you must become a student of human behavior, studying the other's movements, speech patterns, attitude, words, gestures, and expressions to analyze people successfully.

You've been introduced to the nonverbal language and the four main personality types, and to how you form accurate perceptions, but all these things are not separate from one another. They all blend to create effective communications. In the next chapter, you'll be asked to read some scenarios and identify the personality types, nonverbal indicators, and interpret the intended message.

How Can Anyone Read People?

Many things can cloud your judgment when reading people. Biases, intimidation, and sexual attraction are just some of the things that can make you choose to ignore your gut and misread someone. You may think that someone's harsh actions are admirable if you admire the person, while their actions would appear despicable if you did not admire them. Do not let anything cloud your judgment.

Men are more likely to judge pretty young women less harshly. They let pretty young women get away with disrespectful behavior in hopes of winning their favor. If you are attracted to someone, you are more likely to ignore red flags about the person. Try to look past sexual attraction. Understand that there are plenty of attractive people in the world, so fixating on one person's attractiveness is not necessary. You just need to view an attractive person more objectively. Try to focus on his or her character as a separate thing from his or her looks.

Status or certain jobs can also make you admire someone. But understand that someone is not perfect just because of his or her status. Do not let someone's status intimidate you or bamboozle you. They probably got to where they are today by being cruel to others. Read their character separately from their status or work.

Being in your emotional funk can distort your judgment, too. When you are emotionally down, you may be harsher to judge others in your state of bitterness. You may also be more vulnerable to kind actions from others. Unfortunately, manipulators are great at spotting when you are upset and offering a kind action to gain favor with you. Do not let your emotional state make you vulnerable in judgment.

Emotional wounds can make it hard for you to trust people. This is especially true after you have been through a divorce or bad breakup. As a result, you might judge the gender that you are attracted to unfairly. You may instantly dislike all people of that gender. Do not be so quick to write off people that you do not know. Use your scars as lessons to read people who remind you of those that have hurt you in the past, but do not make the mistake of thinking that the entire gender is bad. Give individuals a chance. Try to read them for who they are, not who your ex was.

Don't Just Base it Off of Behavior

Many people make the mistake of trying to read people off of behavior alone. But often behavior offers an incomplete and inaccurate picture.

Often, you cannot know all of this information, so don't even attempt to read someone based on behavior alone.

Sometimes the behavior is inaccurate because it is fake. Many people are great at creating a façade. They appear normal and upstanding while hiding their horrendous internal flaws. Think of most serial killers. Often, they go to work, keep nice houses, and look like totally normal people. The world is shocked when they are finally caught with a basement full of hacked up bodies and torture devices. Sexual deviants who get caught watching child porn are often politicians and businessmen with great jobs and normal outside appearances. While these examples are extreme, many people are adept at hiding their bad personalities under totally normal behavior. Therefore, you cannot base judgments on the outward behavior of others, as this behavior can be faked and misleading.

Create a Baseline

Try to gauge a baseline of someone's normal behavior. Watch for unusual mannerisms that a person often displays. Quirks and habits that you frequently observe in someone over time form the person's baseline. A baseline does not take long to form once you become more adept at reading people with practice. FBI profilers will usually gather this information within the first fifteen seconds of meeting a person.

From this baseline, you can tell when someone is behaving abnormally. When someone is behaving abnormally, you can determine that something is going on. Perhaps the person is lying or is upset about something.

It is difficult to start a baseline on someone if you do not have a chance to observe him over some time and you are not yet adept at reading people in just a few seconds. Therefore, it is a good idea to watch for really odd behavior. Behavior that stands out as unusual may be a quirk or it may be a sign of something more ominous, such as deception. You may want to ask other people who know the person well if this behavior is normal for him. If you can't do that, then you simply must rely on your gut. But do not rely too much on behavior to form judgments about people.

You can start a baseline just by asking someone how they are doing today. Watch how the person reacts. From there, you can determine what his or her normal mannerisms are. The more you talk, the more you can gather about the person's baseline. Does his eye tick often? Does he often gesticulate with his hands? Does he stutter normally, or is he normally articulate? Also, gauge the speed with which he speaks in normal conversation and the tone and pitch of his voice.

You must establish a baseline to tell when someone is behaving inconsistently. Besides, a baseline lets you know how a person is in normal settings. If a person is typically nervous, you can decide if you want to be around someone who is frequently nervous and therefore probably insecure with social anxiety. If a person is typically rude and blunt, you can determine if you want to deal with that kind of behavior in the future.

Infer Things from the Initial Reaction

Of course, strangers tend to be tense in their initial behavior toward you because they do not know you well. But a person's initial reaction to you indicates a lot of information about how he feels about himself and how he feels about other people. This initial reaction shows the hang-ups he may have and the guard that he puts up to protect himself or the façade that he erects to charm people that he meets for the first time. As a result, this reaction says a lot about who he is as a person and the things that you may expect from him as you get to know him better.

If he is initially rude, for instance, he may thaw and become nicer toward you, but you know that at heart he has his guard up against new people. You can then wonder why he has his guard up. He is probably a sensitive and insecure person with a lot of emotional baggage; he feels that he has to act tough and careless to avoid getting hurt.

Particularly articulate and charming people usually have a lot to hide. They are great at being around people and hiding who they are. They have designed behavior that is intended to hook people. Very charming behavior is often indicative of manipulative and deceptive personalities.

An overly nervous person usually has social anxiety and is rife with insecurities. This person will probably get more comfortable with you over time. However, you may want to avoid trusting him too much. As a general rule, insecure people are not reliable and will act in ways that are not always appropriate. Insecure people tend to have trust issues and they will act out in ways that are hurtful because they believe that they are not good enough. You are not responsible for the insecurities of another person, so don't allow such a person to burden you with his problems and doubts.

A person who acts too calm is probably also a sufferer of social anxiety. However, he is adept at projecting calmness to hide how nervous he is. Become suspicious of people who are just "too chill."

Also, watch for people who only want to talk about themselves. People who are obsessed with themselves and don't even try to ask you questions about yourself are typically very selfish. This behavior will not change with time.

Another behavior that will not change with time is someone negative, even in your first meeting. People like this are very toxic and will simply try to drag you down.

A person who talks about others shamelessly when he first meets you is also probably a chronic gossip. It is not normal for someone to start gossiping when he first meets you.

Positivity and enthusiasm are great signs in a person that you have just met. However, if someone talks too much of a big game and brags overly much, you can assume that this person is trying to impress you or even make up for something that he feels that he is lacking. Mild positivity and enthusiasm is a great sign, but being overly enthusiastic is not.

Confidence and assurance of one's self is a good sign in a stranger. A person who is willing to introduce himself to you, look you in the eye, and talk to you is usually secure in himself. He has developed good social skills and hence might be a more sensitive friend, lover, or work associate. While you want to be wary of people who are too smooth and charming, someone who acts normal yet confident is usually a good person to know.

Ask Pointed Questions

If you want to get to know someone, feel free to ask him questions about himself. He will probably volunteer a lot of the information that you want to know. You don't even have to ask him things to find out a lot of information about who he is as a person, what he likes, and what he is looking for from his association with you.

But if he does not volunteer what you want to know, then ask. It is best to ask pointed questions and not be vague. If you are vague, you run the risk of miscommunication. As an adult, there is no use or time for games anymore. You know that you cannot be a mind reader, and neither can anyone else. So, ask what you want to know without shame.

You do not want to appear like you are interrogating someone. Asking rapid-fire questions can put a person off. Asking overly personal questions about someone's life, family, or personality is also off-putting. But do not be afraid to ask general, socially acceptable questions whenever there is a break in the conversation.

Monitor a person in how he answers your questions. Since you have already more or less established a good baseline, you can tell when there are inconsistencies in his responses. If his gestures, tone, pitch, or eye contact suddenly shifts away from his baseline, then you can tell that he is not being truthful or that a question makes him uncomfortable for some reason. You can change the subject or pursue it more, depending on your goal in communication with him.

Word Choice is Important

How a person talks indicates a lot about what he is feeling and thinking. Listen for keywords that indicate his intentions and his basic state of mind. The words that he chooses say a lot about how he is as a human being and what he is feeling at the moment. If you are meeting someone for the first time, remember that the initial meeting speaks volumes about who a person is inside. How he chooses to speak to you right off the bat indicates a lot about who he is generally.

Someone who uses very harsh, aggressive language is an aggressive person, or else he is currently in an angry mood. You never want someone to show you anger when you first meet; this indicates that the person may have an anger management problem.

Someone who uses very vague wording is possibly passive-aggressive and trying to skirt around a hard subject. This type of person is not able to be direct. Expect games and behavior like shirking responsibility. If this person wrongs you, he will probably never admit to it and apologize. If he has a problem with you, he will probably never tell you to your face, but rather will hint about it or tell everyone else how he feels except for you.

Another troubling sign is when someone repeatedly says sorry or seems to take the blame for things. This type of person is very insecure and blames himself for everything.

Someone who uses conceited language, such as bragging about how he just won "another" award, indicates how proud he is of himself. Watch for people who brag too much about themselves. These people are usually narcissistic and egotistical or else they are overcompensating for feelings of inadequacy.

A person who uses very critical language is probably an overly judgmental person or a perfectionist. Watch for someone who nitpicks everything. This is a trait that will not lessen with time. If anything, it will only grow worse with time.

Most people use "I" terms more frequently than any other. This is not a troubling sign, but someone who uses more "we" terms is a better team player who is looking to collaborate with you. Someone who uses more "you" terms is focused on you. This can be a great sign that someone is focused on pleasing you and getting to know you, or else it can be a worrisome sign that someone is trying to manipulate you. Watch for other word choices to tell the difference. If someone is asking you about what you like or who you are, then that is usually a sign that he wants to get to know you or find out how to best please you. This is a great sign on a date, a new friend, or a person that you are thinking about hiring for a service. But if he seems to be fishing for pertinent information with overly personal questions, if he keeps trying to find ways that he can commiserate with you so that you will confide in him, or if he is using fancy language and flattery to make you feel ingratiate and charmed by him, then that is a bad sign that he is trying to get an emotional hook into you to manipulate you.

A good sign that someone is being shifty is vague language. Someone who refuses to answer yes or no questions is probably lying. Someone who uses confusing language is probably deliberately creating a sort of mirage of vagueness to hide something.

How to Detect Romantic Interest in a Moment

Finding out the signs that others are interested in you can be difficult. Does eye contact mean appeal? How about that lady's adorable laugh when you're talking to her? There are also several clear signals to locate if somebody likes you, e.g., eye contact, flirting, and other forms of body language. Know all the important clues to understanding the meaning of that look. Eye contact is among the typical signs of appeal. If you realize that someone is staring at you, there may be indications of attraction. This is also a wonderful way to let others know that you are concerned about them and that you are available; just don't overdo it and look too long.

Attracted Is Attractive

A recent report reveals eye contact research and expressing appeal. Not only does eye contact signal their attractiveness to you, but it also ends up making you feel close to them. Have you ever heard the expression, "It's fascinating to be interested?" In this case, "Attracted is attractive" since it tends to like other people who find it interesting. When the eye contact is given back and retained, the intimacy intensifies. Another sign of emotional connection is dilated pupils. Dilated pupils can make girls even more appealing to guys (it makes them weaker and more ladylike), although the dilated pupils of a guy do not always have the same desirable impact on girls.

Provocative Looks

The appearance on the faces of the people can be a good signal. You can see the flame of a smile, mostly in eye gestures. If an individual is too timid, however, contact with the eyes may be avoided, but when that person grabs your attention, you may realize that it is an opportunity to come and chat. Even though you claim not to care, you can sense him staring at you. You realize that he can't just take his eyes off your face. You may notice that he stares at you and then pulls away swiftly.

Often the easiest way to tell if somebody's interested in you is to give a teasing message and see what's going on. Try to be somewhat more polite to see if your effort is reciprocated by the man. If there is, both people will benefit from that emotional connection and want more. Just ensure that you don't project your appeal to someone else. Give a clear indication and then pull back to find out if it's being taken for granted.

Try Different Flirting Strategies

Flirting does not always come in the form of chuckling and blushing. There are several ways to strike up a conversation. Show your interest in a subtle way to give a person only a little more important than anybody else near you. If you realize that the other person is acting as if you are the only one in the place (regardless of others in there), there is a great possibility that the interaction will begin.

Be Confident

When you are shy, it can be hard to send teasing messages, but know that self-confidence can be appealing. "Fake it until you make it," as the adage goes, and be confident even if you don't feel strong. Expressions According to Psychology Today, if an individual makes a lot of eye contact and leans in or turns their body towards you, it may indicate emotional attachment. They may also show uneasiness in their body language, such as excess twitching or imitating your activities. Generally, you can use a body language-based impression alone to determine whether someone might be interested or not. A few hints are: The person is going to find a reason just to hold you for a moment. He's going to face you continuously. You may feel a strong impression to move closer to the individual based on their gestures.

Nonverbal Flirting

When women are attracted, they frequently giggle during a chat, while guys tend to relax more and prefer to be open and accessible. Research from The Journal of Nonverbal Behavior was explained by the University of Kansas: Male hook-ups (many who think the man must take the initiative) are more relaxed and indulge in nonverbal gestures such as leaning in and holding an open position.

Female hook-ups reveal more of their wrists and hands as they tickle the male delicately. Genuine female hook-ups offer to giggle or smiling playful looks. Both sexes were observant of the object of their emotional connection and abstained from twitching.

Discussion as an Attention-Grabber

A person can be either very sweet or gross when they like you. They seek to have your interest. Often, the person wants to see you always and spend more time alone with you. A suggestion that the person is into you might be to ask you out or make small talk with you. Here are some pointers to look out for: interaction uneasiness, such as instances of shyness or speaking so much.

A person who is casually flirting with you might feel uneasy in one-on-one interactions like you. They hook up better when surrounded by the energy of busy restaurants, bars and clubs, parties and depend more on facial expressions than intimate discussions.

Tickling and trying to be funny are sometimes signs of emotional connection and flirting (genuine flirts can do this, as mentioned above). By inquiring about your mobile number or mail, the individual will want to have private conversations with you.

Unfortunately, it is hard to know when someone is drawn to you or not. Others may be drawn to you as well but decide not to react to it. The easiest thing to do is appreciate yourself and have confidence that the right person will acknowledge you and tell you. Flirt with the ones you're involved in and don't be centered on what happened afterward.

How to Spot an Insecure Person

Today it is accepted that this battle for dominance is a quality of narcissistic character issue. This includes a deviation from the ordinary improvement of one's character, which is changing into an individual who is always looking to raise their confidence. In narcissism, we can discover two sorts of examples: the self-important and the insecure. The pompous narcissist is portrayed by their extroversion, their control, and their quest for fame. The helpless narcissist, then again, is very touchy to analysis or dissatisfaction, to the point that analysis can wind up troubling them.

This damages their social connections because of their steady requirement for esteem. In both of these two cases, when you are with somebody who is making you feel small, it could be due to narcissism and an absence of confidence. Truth be told, even though narcissism doesn't generally ascend to obsessive levels, it is extremely normal.

The Person That Is Insecure Tries to Make You Feel Insecure About Yourself

Once you start questioning your self-worth, it is usually about the type of person who is always expressing his or her abilities. Since you are not always insecure, it is important to watch how you feel when you are around others. You will easily spot an insecure person when you feel a sense of insecurity, which happens when you are around that person who is always talking about his great abilities.

The Insecure Person Wants to Demonstrate His Or Her Achievements

Insecure people have a problem in dealing with their inferiority, which prompts them to show every achievement. People who are always bragging about their fulfilling career, their excellent schooling, or their wonderful kids may well do so to reassure themselves they're really good enough to justify it.

The Insecure Person Tries to Boast Using The 'Humble Mask.'

The mask is a way to hide their vanity. You will find them on Twitter; when a friend whines about all the travel they have to do (because of the value of their job), or all the time they have to spend watching their children play (or, by the way, win) football games.

How to Spot the Liars

The wonder about why people lie is intriguing and incredibly important. Lying is a hard part of human behavior to understand, and it helps to know why people do it and how often it generally happens. And not only why people lie in general, but more importantly, perhaps is the question, why are people lying specifically to you?

Often when people choose to lie, it has more to do with themselves. Yet, in other circumstances, there is something about you that prompts that person to lie to you. This is not always a bad thing though! When another chooses to lie to you it is in the reflection of the best qualities you possess. And these qualities are things you do not and probably should not change. Your best qualities are things you should be proud of and share openly, regardless of the effects it has on others, particularly in terms of lying. However, this information is valuable in recognizing how your premier qualities and strengths can attract lying and liars. Besides, you might possess other qualities, which are not very positive that increase the likelihood that people will lie to you. These more negative qualities might be something you want to develop. Below are a few of the key facts regarding how you may encourage others to lie to you.

Almost all humans are capable and using a form of deceit or lying regularly. It was not until just recently that people began researching this topic further, especially focusing on how often someone lies. According to some survey data, as many as 96% of people admit to at least sometimes lying. Another survey involving more than 1,000 adults in America revealed that 60% of participants said they did not lie at all. In this study, the researchers saw that only 5% of the participants were responsible for more than 50% of the lies told. This particular study says that lying is prevalent, but the group of liars is small. At least, the group of prolific liars is small. But many more surveys have shown that almost all people, close to 95%, lie at some point. The lies can be small "fibs" or "white lies," intended to protect someone. For example, despite thinking the pants someone has on are terrible, you say to them, "no, those pants look fine on you." But in other instances, lying can be more serious and sinister. For example, if someone lies on their job application or is trying to cover up a crime they have committed.

Despite lying being prevalent in human nature, many people are terrible at telling if someone is lying. And on top of that, many people think that they are good at telling if someone is a liar, but they are not. Part of that false belief is that there are old theories people still believe, such as:

- Liars squirm and fidget

- Liars will not make eye contact

- Liars shift their eyes around a lot when they are lying

These are not necessarily true. Yes, there are differences in the behaviors of those telling the truth and those lying, but it can be a challenge to measure the differences and tell them apart. There are some theories on how to tell if someone is lying presented in contemporary research. Based on this research, several indicators can help. But no matter what, the best way to tell someone is lying is to trust your "gut." Your instinct is a powerful tool in this process.

The Body Language of a Liar

Detecting a liar typically means people are focusing on the message body language shares, or the small behavioral and physical indicators that expose deceit. A few of the common ideas include the eyes shifting around, fidgeting constantly, and lack of eye contact. It was believed that these were fool-proof indicators that the person communicating is lying.

Yes, the cues shared through body language can identify deceptions; some research indicates that several of the highly anticipated expressions are not closely tied to lying. Psychologist Howard Ehrlichman, a researcher dedicated to eye movements since the 1970s, revealed that the movement of the eye does not indicate lying at all. Ehrlichman hypothesizes that eyes shifting around reveal that a person is intently thinking, or more accurately, that the person is tapping into how or her long-term memory.

Additional research shows that even though single behaviors and signals are capable of indicating deception and lies, a few of the behaviors commonly connected to deceit, like rapid eye movement, are some of the worst tells. And even though body language can be a valuable method for lie detection, the important piece is to recognize which signs to place value on and which to let go.

The Signs Linked to a Liar

Law enforcement has greatly benefited from psychologists who showed them how body language and deception could help officers identify between lies and the truth. UCLA researchers studied the subject of body language and lying, as well as how to analyze deception to create better training and recommendations for law enforcement. This took more than 60 studies on deception to develop these recommendations. The American Journal of Forensic Psychiatry published the results of these studies.

Red Flags That Someone May Be Lying

Some of the new "red flags" that researchers feel could potentially reveal that people are untrustworthy include:

- Sharing minimal details or being vague
- Before answering the question, the person repeats the question
- Sentence responses are not complete sentences but are rather fragments
- When the story they are telling is challenged that cannot offer certain details to the listener
- "Grooming" habits become more evident, like pressing fingers to his or her lips or touching their hair

Chapter 18: Hypnotic Induction

Hypnosis is a characteristic perspective. It is a state given to us for personal development. There has never been an archived instance of mischief coming to anybody from trance induction's therapeutic utilization is additionally a great sentiment of complete physical and mental unwinding. It is like that second between realizing you are wakeful and going into the rest state.

An individual may decide to remain in spellbinding after an accomplished subliminal specialist requests that they emerge from it. The explanation being, it is quite a casual sentiment of happiness; they want to remain mesmerized for a spell longer. The individual at that point rests and stirs, of course. In self-entrancing, you have full oversight and set your time limit. There has never been a recorded instance of somebody incapable of emerging from spellbinding.

Nobody is mesmerized without wanting to. The hypnotherapist just helps the subject, who mesmerizes himself. Procedures exist by which one can accomplish a condition of self-entrancing and increase total unwinding under the most unpleasant conditions. In this expression, the psyche mind is available to restorative proposals.

When mesmerized, members in a phase show find that their minds become unfathomably incredible. They are glad to do foolish things for a group of people since it is simple to envision and acknowledge the trance specialist's recommendations.

In self-spellbinding, you pick your time limits, understanding that you have a decision and would now be able to choose your region for personal growth. Utilizing spellbinding toward the start of your mindfulness, preparing is of extraordinary advantage. It speeds up the retraining cycle.

Hypnosis is a perspective in which an individual's activities and feelings are controlled through a system of exercises known as spellbinding incitement. The incitement factor can shift from individual to individual and starting with one hypothesis then onto the next. Entrancing relies upon the individual's psychological situation; likewise, the individual who is delivering the upgrade.

Hypnosis has for some time been a topic of conversation and opponent speculations. A portion of the specialists has asserted that spellbinding is a sort of phony medication given to a patient as a strong one. Sometimes, just by expecting the inactive pill's impact, positive changes have been seen in the patients. These specialists accept that spellbinding is a serious type of impact. Then again, there are speculations about spellbinding being associated with the individual's conscious or oblivious brain.

A few people have accepted that we can associate the oblivious brain through spellbinding throughout the century. Ongoing examinations into the mechanics of spellbinding have indicated that the mind's conscious portion is the most associated one during this psychological state. Nonetheless, the discussion on this is continuous throughout the previous twenty years.

Spellbinding has been characterized in a few stages also. The investigations uncover that these classes depend on the physiological pattern, perspective, and state of being of the subject over the section of years. Additionally, it is likewise founded on the devices utilized for animating the cycle of spellbinding.

Hypnosis has been dealt with more like a spiritualist cycle in the course of the last numerous years. As it may, clinical exploration has demonstrated its advantages as it is nowadays engaged with Trauma treatments that hit patients. Whether one calls it sorcery or medication, if its target stays positive, it is valuable, and its training should proceed.

Hypnosis is a specific mental state with explicit physiological traits, looking like rest just cursorily and set apart by a person working at a degree of mindfulness other than the conventional cognizant state. This state is portrayed by a level of expanded openness and responsiveness in which internal experiential observations are given as much criticalness as is commonly offered distinctly to outside the real world.

What Are the Differences Between Hypnosis on Stage And In Real Life?

Hypnotherapy Vs. Stage Hypnosis

In the realm of spellbinding, there are various kinds of trance specialists and 'subgenres.' However, all things considered, you can classify the employment of entrancing into two unmistakable gatherings: treatment and diversion. When a resident considers entrancing, he thinks about a phase trance inducer, "transforming individuals into chickens" and so forth, or they accept that a trance specialist helps individuals with killing undesirable conduct and accomplish their objectives utilizing spellbinding.

Overall, in case someone hasn't experienced enchanting for both redirection and treatment, they will, as a rule, consider perhaps by the same token. Like this, it is exceptionally normal for new hypnotherapy clients to ask their subconscious authorities quickly before the start of the treatment meeting, "... you're not going to make me a chicken, are you?" Given that hypnotherapy and stage hypnotizing are exceptional, they frequently pack them into one tremendous class of enchanting. Genuinely, stage hypnotizing and hypnotherapy are extraordinary, yet there are likenesses too.

Differentiations

For sure, the essential difference between stage hypnotizing and hypnotherapy is the typical outcome. Stage daze pros need to present a show and give volunteers and the group fun and drawing as expected. Similarly, subconscious stage authorities give suggestions that sole prop up for the range of the show and are dispensed with after the volunteers are 'blended' at the end.

On the other hand, a subconscious authority needs to help clients achieve an individual goal, be it more confidence, halting smoking, resting better, shedding pounds, or various things a client may need to go after. The daze inducer gives a proposition intended to remain past the gathering ('post-entrancing suggestions'), so the client experiences a drawn-out change in various pieces of their life.

This way, one's for redirection, and the spellbinding proposals are temporary. The other is for long stretch personal change and improvement.

Is That the Same?

Surely, the aftereffects of hypnotherapy and stage enchanting are profoundly exceptional, yet countless the systems and approaches used can be on a very basic level equivalent to, if not indistinct. For instance, both stage daze authorities and subconscious pros use 'spellbinding acknowledgments' to entrance their clients/volunteers.

These can be "snappy selections" or "all the more moderate reformist acknowledgments," and the stage daze inducer or the subconscious expert can uphold the two philosophies. Hypnotizing is enchanting, whether or not it is used for redirection or treatment; the state of fascinating is the same. A couple of individuals have all the earmarks of being essentially enchanted than others, yet this is ordinarily a consequence of their receptivity to a hypnotizing proposition rather than the specific strategies used.

Regarding receptivity, suggestibility, and testing/significance are various resemblances between stage enchanting and hypnotherapy. Subconscious masters benefit by knowing how suggestible a volunteer or client is, as it can contact what the trance inducer taught them to do or what likely won't be plausible for said individual.

A stage daze inducer uses suggestibility testing to pick their volunteers (requiring only the most open people from the group). Curiously, a subconscious authority may use comparative tests as a 'warm-up' for the customer or figure out which kind of approaches or recommendations to use or avoid during the treatment meeting.

Concerning happens after someone is spellbound (the treatment or the lovely stuff), a comparative technique is used (really, truly). That technique is called 'proposition.' All subconscious masters and daze inducers use contemplations to make and direct their subjects' experiences.

A stage trance specialist gives suggestions for a volunteer to 'imagine that you are clung to the seat' or 'notice that possibly your shoe is a telephone, and it's ringing, so you ought to get it.'

In like manner, a daze authority may give suggestions for a client to 'imagine looking at yourself in a mirror, seeing the overhauled you that you will be or to observe. That is like that old affinity for smoking has recently moved into the past, and now it's essentially something that you used to do alrcady. The glamorous stage proposals are intended to inspire a more physical/outer reaction from the spellbound volunteers (for individuals to watch). Interestingly, the hypnotherapy recommendations are expected to make a more mental/natural reaction inside the customer (to make changes). Toward the day's end, however, they're all still recommendations.

What Are the Advantages of Hypnotizing Someone?

The Benefits of Controlling Other People

When most people want to learn to hypnotize, they imagine people acting ridiculous on command for the amusement of others or someone lying on a couch while a psychotherapist puts them to sleep.

But hypnosis is simply a heightened state of awareness that opens the mind to seeds of suggestion. When you learn to hypnotize and become a skilled covert hypnotist, you'll know how to take advantage of this receptive state of mind.

When you learn to hypnotize, you lead people to believe that they're following your commands of their own free will. You lead them to think that it was their idea to give you that promotion, buy you that pricey piece of jewelry, or have dinner with you.

Because you're speaking directly to their unconscious mind, they don't even realize what's happening. It doesn't have to be on a sidewalk at a state fair or in a therapist's office.

It can be utilizing one of the most powerful forces that exist between two people: Language. It's not just what you say, but how you say it - and it's not only verbal language, it's body language. And people who learn to hypnotize have realized this.

Imagine being able to change your life through the power of hypnosis. Learn to hypnotize, and you learn to get what you want from people who don't even realize what you're doing.

What are your objectives? What are your goals? What kind of hypnotist do you want to be? If you're like most people, you simply want to guide people in the direction you want them to go. And once you learn to hypnotize, you'll be able to do just that!

Human beings only use about 10 percent of their brainpower. When you learn to hypnotize, you take the first steps toward understanding the mind's full strength.

Once you're able to break into the various dimensions of a person's subconscious, you can start a romance, prosper professionally, and improve your quality of life by tackling the elusiveness of one single life ability - control.

In today's busy world, most of us feel like we're losing grasp of our families, relationships, jobs, and sometimes even ourselves. Imagine being able to regain not only self-control but the ability to influence those around you through covert mind control and underground hypnosis.

Chapter 19: Techniques of Dark Psychology

Now, the reason why dark psychology techniques are effectively lying in the way they interact with your psyche. The human psyche is structured to filter out stimuli that somehow don't conform to the patterns, beliefs, and values that permeate the psyche. For instance, if you believe in peace, your mind will reject any notion of violence. By the same token, if your mind is centered on greed and avarice, you may place minimal restrictions on schemes aimed at getting money.

However, the subconscious mind, the layer that exists beneath the conscious mind, is unfiltered but equally able to process the stimuli that enter it. This is why the manipulator's true goal is to access your subconscious and implant ideas at that level. When that happens, the chances of ideas and beliefs sticking are very high.

This is why advertising is so repetitive. Think about it. If you only hear an advert once, the chance of you recalling it would be very slim. However, if you hear adverts over and over, there will come the point where your conscious mind will stop putting up a fight. When that occurs, the message can seep through into your subconscious. This is the secret of brand positioning. So, if you think advertising, at least good advertising anyway, is about selling stuff, guess again. Good advertising is all about getting you to think about a brand or a product constantly.

The Door in The Face!

Directly from the experience of door-to-door salespeople, I present the technique of the door... in the face! When we want to obtain a certain result from our interlocutor, we should request that we consider too high and unreasonable: a metaphorical door will undoubtedly follow this request in the face, that is a refusal; at this point, we should immediately follow the real request that we had in mind: compared with the first the new request will appear more modest and reasonable.

This technique bases its effectiveness on the natural tendency of our minds to make comparisons. If we provide the right term of comparison, no request will appear excessive.

This technique works because it arouses in the person a sense of guilt and an idea of concession. In other words, your renunciation will be perceived as a concession, and then, it is a sneaky application of the "reciprocity rule."

Foot in The Door

This tactic is implemented in increments. This begins with the manipulator asking for small favors. Every time the victim complies, the manipulator will ask for increasingly bigger favors until they get what they ultimately want or exhaust their victim. At that point, the manipulator needs to move on to a fresh victim.

Consider this example:

A manipulator wants a large sum of money. Yet, they know they won't get it if they just ask for it. So, they ask for a tiny sum. Then, they pay it back. After, they ask for a bigger sum and then pay it back. They do this as they build up trust capital until one day; they get what they want, never to be heard from again.

This example clarifies why this technique is called put your "foot in the door" and make room with your whole body...

A more rudimentary approach consists of asking multiple people for money with no intention of paying it back. Eventually, they exhaust the people around them. So, they need to move on and find new victims.

In the "foot in the entryway" method, more modest solicitations are approached to pick up consistence with bigger solicitations, while the strategy "entryway in the face" works the other way, where bigger solicitations are asked, with the desire that it will be dismissed, to pick up consistence for more modest solicitations.

"Yes-Set" Technique

The "yes-set" technique consists of asking several questions to the interlocutor, for which he can only agree and answer "yes." This will create light conditioning that will also make him answer yes to your real request. It is a short-term freezing effect that causes the person to enter into a certain response perspective.

4 or 5 harmless questions in the preamble are enough.

For example, you want to watch a specific program on TV, knowing that the choice of your partner will probably be very different:

YOU: It was nice today, huh? It feels good to get some sun!

HIM/HER: Yes, it was.

YOU: Are you watching TV tonight?

HIM/HER: Well, yes, I think so.

YOU: Remember the movie we saw the day before yesterday?

HIM/HER: Yes.

YOU: I liked it. He was practically the main actor, right?

HIM/HER: Yes, he was.

YOU: Do you agree to watch the 1:00 movie tonight? I think it'll be okay.

HIM/HER: Yes, if you want, what is it?

A funny little demonstration of this principle that I'm sure you already know. Ask someone to repeat the word "white" 10 times, and then ask the question, "What is the cow drinking?" The wrong answer will have been conditioned by past repetition.

This technique's mechanism is based on the use of "rhetorical questions" or statements that are true, taken for granted, or otherwise verifiable in the person's direct experience.

In these cases, the person "leading" the report prepares the ground with a series of questions to which the interlocutor will surely answer yes, which is why it is called "Yes-Set."

And in all three cases, some truisms or true and verifiable statements are followed by an "unverifiable statement" called an induction (or command) or a demand taken for granted.

Linguistic Presupposition

Some very insidious communicative maneuvers consist of asking the interlocutor questions to which it is impossible to answer simply with a "YES" or a "NO," but that trigger in the subject of the actions as an answer to a command. For example, if I ask a person if he "can turn off the light, there on his right?" apparently, I am asking if he can do it, but I will get the switch off in practice, which is actually what I wanted.

In other words, through the linguistic form of "embedded commands," you can skillfully camouflage a command into a question, as in the following example: "Do you want to tell me what's bothering you or would you rather wait a while?"

With this sentence, I create in practice an alternative through the construction of more proposals, where I take for granted that in any case, the subject will reveal to me what worries him.

Linguistic-Presupposition is one of the most powerful and easy to use tools to give someone "apparently" a choice and, at the same time, "trap" them inside your idea, almost without any way out.

Bind is a hypnotic technique used to force a choice with words. It is also called the "illusion of alternative."

Let's see some examples:

- "After you go to buy bread, could you come by the newsstand and buy me the paper?"

- "When are you going to take me to the movies?"

- "Have you decided which foreign country to take me to for our anniversary?"

Each of these questions already provides a choice, and the trick is to take for granted a fact that is slightly hidden.

Reverse Psychology

This technique consists of assuming a behavior opposite to the desired one, with the expectation that this "prohibition" will arouse curiosity and therefore induce the person to do what is desired. For instance, when you tell a child not to do something, that is the first thing they do. This type of response persists throughout a person's life.

It's a way of getting things done, giving the opposite of the command you want. If I say things like, "don't be offended" "don't worry," I get the opposite effect. I will make my interlocutor stiffen.

Some people are known to be like boomerangs because they refuse to go in the direction, they are sent but take the opposite route. A dark persuader can use this type of behavior because it is a weakness that the victim has. Take an example of a friend who loves to eat junk food at any opportunity they get. The dark persuader knows this and therefore will suggest that they should eat healthy because it will be good for them, knowing that the friend will choose fast food anyway.

When individuals are told that they should not believe one thing or the other, they will pay closer attention.

Consider this situation:

You are looking to force your employees to work overtime without questioning it. However, getting them to log the hours can be challenging as no one is keen on staying beyond their usual shift. So, you really can't do much to convince them to work overtime.

Then, you get an idea: Why not ban overtime? That is, anyone who wants to work overtime cannot do so. The justification behind it is that since no one wants to stay longer hours, there will be no overtime. You could take it a step further and hire temp workers to fill in the extra hours. Now, your regular staff is concerned that others are infringing upon their jobs. In the end, you may get resistance from your usual staff who are now demanding to work overtime to get rid of the temp workers.

In the end, you have successfully manipulated your staff to work overtime. You were able to play with their sense of security by banning overtime and then bringing other workers to cover the hours they wouldn't.

A convention playbook would have sought to incentivize workers to be more willing to stay longer hours. But this would have meant paying more or offering greater benefits. In the end, your manipulation attempts were successful without conceding any additional benefits.

Negative Hidden Commands

A negative hidden command is a specific linguistic model of reverse psychology in which instruction is formulated negatively so that it is perceived by the unconscious mind, bypassing the "critical guardian" of our interlocutor.

An interesting aspect of the unconscious mind is that it does not understand negation than the conscious one. This happens because our mind works by images and because there is no mental representation of the word "NOT." Therefore, the unconscious does not perceive it. In other words, our brain cannot deny experiences related to the senses without first visualizing them.

Generally, in Guerrilla Marketing, NLP, the psychology of communication, and neuro-marketing, two examples are given below to explain this concept.

1.Read the following sentence and do what it says: "Don't think of a pink elephant."

What were you thinking? Almost certainly a pink elephant, even though you were asked not to.

2.Now I ask you not to think of a yellow lemon. Think about what you want, but don't think of a yellow lemon. Don't think of a big, juicy yellow lemon, its intense aroma, its sour taste. Don't think about cutting the yellow lemon in two, squeezing half of it in your mouth, and drinking its sour juice.

Chapter 20: Understanding Deception

Dark or Not?

Deception is a critical part of dim brain research. In the same way as other dim mental strategies, it very well may be hard to tell if any given case of trickiness is dim. Before we investigate the distinction between dull and typical trickiness, we should initially see precisely what duplicity is.

Many individuals would express the perspective that lying and trickiness are something very similar. This is mistaken. Lying is a type of trickery; however, it is in no way, shape, or forms the main structure duplicity can take. Instead of considering double-dealing "lies," it is smarter to consider it "misdirecting." Any activity or word equipped for causing somebody to think some different option from reality can be precisely named trickery.

So, what are some basic signs of trickiness? Lying, excluding reality, inferring misrepresentation, or deceitfully giving proof to something bogus are largely tricky instances. You will likely understand that you have done a portion of these things, eventually yourself. Does that imply that all demonstrations of duplicity are instances of dull brain research? Not in any way.

Everybody tricks somewhat or another. Individuals may trick others for a scope of reasons, for example, consideration, humiliation, or sentiments of insufficiency. For instance, contemplates have demonstrated that many men will lie about their stature on dating sites. This doesn't make them experts of dull brain science! Individuals even fool themselves about the scope of issues, including their wellbeing, aspiration, and satisfaction. Such everyday instances of duplicity don't compare to dim trickery.

Trickiness can be viewed as dim when done with either an adverse or detached expectation toward the hoodwinked individual. Powerlessness generally propels typical trickery to look up to reality somehow. Then again, Dim duplicity agrees that reality doesn't serve the tricky points of the double-crosser. Hence, the fact of the matter is either changed, covered up, or overlooked for a rendition of occasions that better suits the motivation behind the individual misdirection.

Set forth plainly, individuals who send dim brain research use duplicity to hurt, not assistance. They help their advantages, however, at any cost, paying little heed to who gets injured.

A few people accept that if duplicity is the little scope, it can't be viewed as dull, while bigger double-dealings must be inalienably dim. This isn't the situation. By investigating the possibility of the double-dealing range, you will see that it isn't the duplicity size that decides if it is dull or not, rather the reason behind the trickiness.

The Deception Spectrum

To comprehend the possibility of misdirection, comprehend that it can happen on either an enormous or a small scope. One of the principles messes up that individuals frequently expect that trickiness is just genuine if it is huge and doesn't make a difference if it is little. This is a grave mistake. Little duplicities can be utilized in an intensely dim manner by gifted controllers and are regularly more viable than enormous trickeries. The absolute biggest double-dealings ever are done by purposeful controllers to serve their points and goals. Dull instances of different kinds of misdirection, huge and little, will currently be introduced to outline the possibility of the trickery range.

So, what is a portion of the manners in which more modest trickeries can be utilized by individuals who practice the craft of dim brain research? Regularly, little misdirections are utilized to test the casualty's naïveté and condition them into accepting the controller's beguiling explanations and activities. If individuals are molded to accept a scope of more modest lies after some time, they are bound to accept a bigger lie later on. This progressive molding isn't the main way more modest trickeries can be utilized as a dull mental weapon.

More modest double-dealings can likewise be completed to sabotage a casualty's trust in their forces of rationale and reason. Suppose a controller tricks a casualty over minor issues, and the casualty starts to address what's going on. In that case, the casualty may well presume that their doubt is silly, and they consequently can't confide in their judgment. Many people are bound to infer that their judgment is defective, as opposed to someone else is misleading them over minor issues. Clients of dim brain science know about this general "trust" that individuals have and misuse it without leniency.

Enormous scope trickery can likewise be an illustration of dim brain research, practically speaking. Perhaps the biggest trickiness conceivable is to persuade somebody that you are an unexpected individual compared to what you say you are. Not regarding the character or some other detail. A whole personality. Name, date of birth, everything! The most talented clients of dim brain research can convince others to purchase totally into their depiction of a bogus personality and foundation.

Since it has been demonstrated how manipulative clients of dull brain science can utilize the trickery range for their points, we will probably investigate the most well-known themes, and subjects' individuals are bamboozled about. At that point, we will take a gander at precisely how these huge and little scope duplicities are completed by investigating the particular strategies that are utilized.

Signs of Deception

Deception is similar to lying, but it has some different components. One of them is equivocation. Equivocation is when someone makes vague or ambiguous statements. The point is to make things unclear, not to point out the mistake in their logic. Deception is making things seem a certain way when they are not that way. Deception is when a person uses any tactics to help make a situation seem different than it is. Lying by omission is one example of this. Lying by omission is when a person leaves out important information for the sake of changing others' perception of reality. Deception is done without a person's knowledge. It changes their perception of the situation without actually lying. Camouflage is another example of this deception technique. This happens when someone is trying to hide the truth to realize that they are missing some of the story's necessary parts. This will be used when someone is employing half-truths. Camouflage will happen when somebody is trying to hide their real name or what they do for work. Camouflaging can be conceptualized as a way to hide in plain sight, in metaphorical terms. A skilled person in employing camouflage will change their entire persona, including body language, when necessary.

One unique, more specific strategy often used in Dark Persuasion is the "give and take." The give and take technique works by fitting you into a dialogue about whatever the subject matter at hand is. The "give and take" technique works because a trick people into thinking that they are actually in an equal relationship when they are not. People tend to trust those with whom they engage in a back-and-forth. They start to think that they are in an honest relationship because there is a feedback loop. This is often not the case. One way to do this is to ask for someone to do a small favor for you. Once they have done the small favor, you then require that they do something else for you. Once both of these are completed, you pay them back. This might be by doing a small favor for them. It might be by offering some kind of material response, like money. Money is one of the biggest motivators for humans living in our time. Now, by establishing this loop of the give and take, you have established a relationship.

Deception, alongside fraud, confusion, imagination, misleading, and beguilement, is a show used to spread emotions in the subject about contortions or almost the whole way feelings. Deception can consolidate a collection of things, such as disguise, spread, impedance, capable deception, presentation, and dissimulation. The director will decide to control the subject's cerebrum, considering how the subject will trust them. The subject will recognize what the ace is communicating and may even be basing reachable plans. Forming their reality depends on what the expert has been letting them know.

On the off chance that the master is rehearsing the deception methodology, they tell the subject will be counterfeit. Trust can, without a considerable amount of a stretch, be pummeled once the subject discovers, which is the clarification the ace must be gifted at the technique of deception and exceptional at getting something moving if they need to proceed with their subject.

Typically, deception will develop the degree that affiliations can incite sentiments of vulnerability and unfaithfulness between the two partners in the relationship. This is considering how deception hurts the rules of most affiliations and is in like way observed to impact the needs that go with that relationship. A considerable number of people need to choose to have a real discussion with their embellishment; if they have discovered that their partner is surprising, they would need to understand how to use confusion and impedance to get the solid and reasonable data that they need. In some way, the trust would be gone from the relationship, making it difficult to develop the relationship back to where it had once been. The subject would dependably be exploring what the ace was outlining for them, thinking about whether the story was authentic, or something made up. Because of this new vulnerability, most affiliations will end once the subject finds a couple of arrangements concerning the master's deception.

Some of the signs of deception are:

The Lack of Self-Reference

If a person is truthful, they will utilize the pronoun "I" when describing what took place. For example, an honest person will go ahead and say, "I arrived home and went straight to the bedroom. After that, I went to talk to my mother, and we had a lengthy chat." That's just an example statement. As we can see, the pronoun "I" appears twice in the statement provided.

Deceptive people will use language that minimizes the number of "I" references. During an oral statement, the witness or suspect may leave out some important information; this can happen even when issuing an informal written statement.

Answering A Question with A Question

Even though a person may be a liar, they will prefer not to engage in the act of lying. When a person lies, they risk being detected. Before you answer a question with a lie, you should avoid answering the question at all costs. When trying to act dodgy, people may often answer a question with another question. The investigators should always be on the lookout for people that answer a question with another question.

Tips used in spotting a liar.

Focus on Building Rapport

It is evident that a "good cop" will always display better results than a "bad cop." During an interview, a person may appear as empathetic, and they will gain access to more information than the person who appears cold. It is also advisable to avoid being accusatory during the interrogation process.

Surprising the Suspects

A deceptive individual will always try to anticipate your next move after a move. For instance, they may try to anticipate your question so that they can ensure each answer they are issuing seems natural. You should always ask those questions that they do not expect.

Listening More Than You Speak

If you are a liar, you will focus on speaking more, and your main goal is to ensure that you will sound legitimate. Also, you will focus on winning over a certain target audience. Some liars may make use of some complex sentences so that they can conceal the truth.

You should be aware of the following things:

When people are stressed, they tend to speak faster.

A stressed person will speak louder.

The liars usually clear their voice and cough regularly, which means that they are experiencing some tension.

Although the statements that have been mentioned above are supposed to enlighten you on how to spot a liar, it is good to note that some people may exhibit some signs of tension, but that is not an indicator that they are lying to you. In case you have noticed any of the mentioned actions, you should proceed with caution.

Pay Attention to How A Person Says "No"

When engaging a suspect, you should pay close attention to how they utter the word "No." A person depicting some unusual behavior will always face another direction as they say, "No." They may also appear hesitant, and they can also close their eyes.

Watch for The Changes in Behavior

When a person changes their behavior, it is an indicator that they may be engaging in deceptive behavior. You should be careful when a person issues some short answers to different questions. Also, they may pretend that they are suffering from memory lapse, especially in a critical moment. They can also start to speak formally, and they may start issuing some exaggerated responses.

Always Ask for The Story Backward

If a person is indeed truthful, they will add some details. They will focus on remembering more stories about what happened. A liar will start by memorizing the story, and they will stick to one narrative. If they add some details, you will notice that they are not adding up by taking a close look at the details. If you suspect someone is deceptive, you should ask them to recall the event in a backward manner, rather than issuing the narrative from the beginning to the end. You can ask them to talk more about what happened right before a certain point. A person who is telling the truth will usually recall many details. A liar will simplify the story, and they will also contradict themselves.

Beware of The Compliments Issued by People

Although compliments are good, they are only good if a genuine person has issued them. You should always be on the lookout for a person who is trying to make a good impression. When you agree with all the opinions being issued by a person and also laugh at all their jokes, it is an indicator that you may be insincere.

Asking A Follow-Up Question

People do not like dealing with liars; however, it is good to remember that sometimes people are uneasy with some questions since they avoid personal embarrassment. Also, some people may be extremely dependent on the outcome of a specific conversation.

For instance, during a job interview, a person may be tempted to hide the details about why they may have been fired from their past job. Although the person may be qualified and their personality is good, they may hide some of these details since they need a job. During the interview, a person may issue a response that may seem puzzling. If you are puzzled during an interview by some of the responses, you can develop some follow-up questions. If you are in doubt, you can continue to ask questions. With time, you will be able to spot whether a person is deceptive or not.

Chapter 21: Speed-Reading People

Speed-reading people takes practice and experience. However, many of the skills you may need to develop may be skills you already have. When you look at a person to sum them up in your mind, you evaluate their body language in a split second; you perceive their facial expression, posture, and actions.

To speed read people effectively, you'll need to be well-versed in the practice of mindfulness. Mindfulness is being aware of the present moment without judging. This is a setup that allows for three parts to include in mindfulness. They are being present, being here and now, and being non-judgmental. Being aware is just letting yourself take in all of the sensory information you have and accept your state. The second part is about being in the present moment, whenever and wherever you are. This can apply to people who often find themselves caught up in their heads; the third part is about non-judging. Non-judging is important because acceptance is a significant motivator in our lives. You must cultivate mindfulness to speed read people because it is the modality you can be comfortable in reaching people's signs and observable cues.

Start cultivating mindfulness by practicing. First, you can just sit in a comfortable position, with your body relaxed, just letting yourself feel your butt in the chair and your feet on the floor. You can do a variety of exercises, including a body scan. The body scan should start at one end of the body, like the head or toes, and go slowly to the other end of the body. This is just directing your attention to different parts of the body and feeling them and noticing what they are doing and what is going on. Direct your attention first at your toes, and just feel what they are feeling. You can feel the clothing they are touching, your socks, or shoes, or you can notice the ground beneath them. This will let you be more in touch with what is happening in your body.

You can also start by just paying attention to the breath. Just place your attention on the physical sensations of the breath. This is just a way to tune into the body and let you be in touch with the body. As you notice each breath, count to ten over and over again. See how high you can count up without losing your attention on one single bodily function. This is a practice that will help you with concentration and attention.

Mindfulness will let you be in the present moment when you are interacting with people and observing them. Being mindful means being aware, and this is your goal when you are trying to speed people. It is to be aware of their posture, body language, and other cues that are very important in analyzing people.

Concentration and attention are essential when you want to speed read people. You will need to employ attention and direction at a particular person when you are speed reading them. You must not appear to be outwardly focusing much of your attention on them, but instead neutrally observing them. First, you can notice their posture. Are they standing up straight? Are they crouched or leaning to one side? It can tell you about the physical state of their body. Older people will have a slightly more hunched over perspective. With younger people, a hunch can mean different things. It can tell that they want themselves to be smaller and less noticeable, and maybe they don't like to be in the public eye. It might betray a sense of shyness in them, that they are not willing to stand up and look people in the eye.

People's sitting posture will tell you a great deal about them as well. Most people who are very mindful try to engage in proper posture most of the time because poor posture can cause the bones to weaken and results in all sorts of health problems. When someone is sitting up in a healthy and attentive posture, you know they are reliable. They take care of their bodies, and they are intentional about this. Sometimes, sitting posture will not be the best indicator, and sometimes, this can throw you off.

What do we mean by effect? The effect is the way that the face is expressing thoughts and feelings. An average impact is considered one with a wide range of expressions, for example, smiling when one is happy and having facial expressions that match what one is saying and doing. The effect is a big clue to how someone is feeling. People with some mental illness, for example, have flat products. It means that their impact does not change very much when they say different things, and they're not able to express feelings with their faces. It comes with a variety of conditions. However, much less severe cases of restricted effect can come from being shy or anxious, or sad. A person may restrict their impact when they have social anxiety, for example. A person's thoughts can be wildly swinging all over the place, and their face is displaying a neutral, calm reaction. It can be a protective mechanism for some people when they hide their emotions. You and other people don't have to deal with the messy reality of where your feelings are. Some people display all of their feelings on their faces. When speed reading people, you just have to determine who much a person's effect represents their feelings. Then, you can engage. Eye contact is a massive part of this. How much eye contact is the person making? Is it sustained and intimate? Is it broken up? Sometimes, people can be aggressive with eye contact, and it can be a way for people to act out their dominance in a situation.

Eye contact is a proximal thing that can connect and divide people. The term "Male gaze" was coined to describe the interaction in eye contact or gaze alone. The male gaze is because of the power of the eye. It is something that we often forget, but eye contact is a powerful tool when you make eye contact with someone. You are making a connection. This connection might frighten some people, and people who are shy or have self-esteem problems will often avoid eye contact to a high degree. This is because they don't trust themselves, and they don't have confidence. A person with confidence can make eye contact with anyone they encounter and engage with. People might be intimidating, but you can always engage with someone in good faith and have confidence in yourself to effectively represent yourself and your ideas.

The only way to start speed reading people is by practicing. Give yourself some practice: go down to the corner store and buy a small thing or two. Look around and see who you see. If there is no one else, practice using the cashier, ask them how their day was, and see how they react. As you are going through this experience, try to pick up as much as you can. Try to focus on them, without lingering, and try to read into the person's body language and effect. You might notice something that you have never seen before.

When you get home, start writing. Start writing what you saw, what the person looked like, whom they acted, and everything else. Start to describe how you felt in your body when interacting with this person and see if you noticed any changes when interacting with you. Some important things to look out for are eye contact, facial expression, body language, and any other vibes you can pick up. Start writing all that you notice and see how much you can glean.

It can be assumed that you have at least some genuine curiosity and interest in your fellow human beings. This is critical in learning how to analyze people effectively. When analyzing people, you will need to do so with a positive, curious, and objective attitude. You will need to listen closely, observe and compare appearance and behavior, and then carefully analyze everything you hear and see to discern a personality pattern.

There are four rules you will need to follow to analyze people reliably:

- Read body language, voice, and general appearance in clusters
- Pay attention to context
- Stay objective
- Keep an eye out for congruent patterns
- Read body language, voice, and general appearance in clusters

People make a very easy and very common mistake when first starting to analyze people is taking a single, isolated piece of information and extrapolating a personality based on that one thing. For example, if an insurance salesman is talking to you and scratches their head, it would be a colossal mistake to assume that the head scratch meant that the salesman was lying. A head scratch, after all, can have a multitude of meanings. For instance, maybe the salesman is forgetful, maybe he has lice, maybe it's uncomfortably hot outside, and he is sweating, maybe the salesman is not quite certain about the answer to a question, maybe the salesman has dandruff or fleas, or perhaps your initial suspicion is correct, and the salesman is lying. The point is that one sole indicator does not give you nearly enough information to get an accurate read on someone.

It is helpful to think of human analysis as learning another language. People are constantly exchanging nonverbal signals.

Like any other language, the language of nonverbal communication has punctuation, words, and sentences. Every gesture, inflection, and piece of clothing should be seen as a word in a sentence, and anyone word can have various meanings.

For example, if I were to ask you to define the word 'set,' for me, what would your response be? 'Set' has over four-hundred possible meanings in the English language depending on the context, so you would probably need more information before offering any kind of reliable definition. Words need to be put into sentences to act concerning other words if you want to get any reliable meaning out of them.

Similarly, nonverbal information also gets communicated in a type of sentence that we will call 'clusters.' Just as you need at least three words to form a sentence in English and thereby reliably interpret any word therein, you generally should try not to analyze someone until you have factored in at least three pieces of information, namely, you should look at what the person's body language is telling you, what the person's voice is telling you, and what the person's general appearance is telling you. Once you have these three elements of your 'sentence,' you can then match the nonverbal cluster up against the actual words that the person has spoken to draw a reliable conclusion.

Pay Attention to Context

All communication needs to be interpreted in the environment, or context, in which it occurs to ensure any kind of accuracy. Think of points on a scatter plot.

If the scatter plot only had a single dot, you would not determine which way the trend was moving because you would not have enough information. This principle applies to human beings as well.

For example, imagine someone sitting down with their arms tightly folded across their chest and their chin down.

Imagine also that the person is shaking one leg up and down very rapidly, speaking in an inconsistent tone and rhythm, and avoiding eye contact.

If the police were interrogating this person, one could safely deduce that the person is lying. However, if the person is waiting at an outdoor bus stop during the winter, it is more likely that this person is simply cold.

And if sitting in the waiting room of a hospital, this person probably is not lying or cold but is most likely nervous or ill. Similarly, if you told me that a man in his mid-twenties had a tattoo, I would not be able to tell you what that means without more information. If the man was in the armed forces, and the tattoo reflects that, the person might conform. If the person is an office manager, he could be of the rebellious type. If he plays in some kind of band, maybe he's trendy. If he's at a carnival with his children, the tattoo may be temporary.

The point is that context is fundamental when determining the meaning of a person's nonverbal communication.

Every aspect of an individual's vocal qualities, words, personal appearance, and body language has many interpretations, so you will need to interpret each in light of the circumstances under which they occur. If you fail to consider when developing your analysis, you are not engaging in analysis but guesswork.

Stay Objective

You cannot analyze people accurately unless you do so objectively. Ironically, the more significant a conclusion is, the more strenuous the task of staying objective becomes due to the emotionality involved.

Further, people generally come to conclusions based on what will be beneficial or detrimental to them in the immediate future, rather than based on a rational consideration of all the available evidence. To avoid bad experiences, the human mind tends to remain blind to truths that it sees as threatening.

The first thing to do to remain objective is to bypass your inclination to avoid facts that you dislike. You can do this simply by understanding the things that may upset you and why. By understanding your triggers in this way, you will be far better prepared for your reaction should those things crop up.

Four mental states often lead to decreased objectivity. We tend to lose our objectivity when we are emotional.

When you meet someone for the first time, take note of three or four most obvious characteristics, such as the person's clothes, quality of speech, voice, size, or mannerisms. This analysis will give you your first impression of a person. But keep in mind that first impressions are simply impressions you got from the person initially. You should constantly measure additional information up to your first impression to watch for developing patterns and pay special attention to new information inconsistent with your first impression. Any inconsistencies may lead you to a different conclusion than the one you initially reached.

Exaggerated Traits

The importance of any particular trait is directly related to how subtle, big, small, or intense it is.

The importance of a trait, then, is a matter of extremes. However, you will generally not accurately gauge any particular trait's significance until after you have learned enough about a person to see a developing pattern. When you are on the lookout for a pattern, pay particular attention to other characteristics or traits consistent with those that are the most dramatic. For example, you may see an obese man and automatically assume that he is self-conscious about his weight. But if upon speaking with him, you find that his body language is open, he has a big booming voice, and he makes self-deprecating jokes, you may have to revise your first impression.

Look for Inconsistency

Any unusual trait or characteristic is significant when analyzing people. There are two classes of deviations.

The first class of deviation consists of traits that conflict with others. We will call these deviations 'rebel traits.'

The second class of deviation is behavior that is out of keeping with an individual's usual routine or habit. We will call these deviations 'rebel actions.'

When you come across a rebel trait, it needs to be scrutinized.

Once in a while, the rebel trait offers a glimpse into the person's real nature when they have successfully hidden every other clue of that reality.

Most often, though, the outlying trait allows you to gain insight into a personality's intricacies rather than its veracity. For example, a successful person in business that is particularly conservative, organized, and well-dressed would indicate a pattern of confidence and professionalism. If this person also wears a bracelet made by his children, that bracelet would be a rebel trait.

This would indicate that in addition to the poise and professionalism of this person's habit, his family is extremely important.

More revealing than rebel traits, however, are rebel actions. We are all creatures of routine and habit. We will ordinarily stick to our usual routines unless something out of the ordinary happens, forcing us to break with that routine. If your neighbor is usually a chatterbox but suddenly starts ignoring you, you will know something is up.

If your spouse usually calls to let you know that they are working late and then begins to neglect those calls, it would be worth asking about. Do not get paranoid, though. A single deviation from an ordinary routine should not rock the foundations of the pattern you have observed, although you should pay attention to it. Regardless of the reason behind it, rebel actions will more than likely help you to gain a more well-rounded understanding of an individual's general personality.

Conclusion

Dark psychology is the investigation of the psyches of the most egregious, enormous people that exist. At the point when you are investigating the profundities of dim brain research, you are investigating the psyches of the individuals who are out to hurt others. Chronic executioners, ace controllers, and victimizers the same may share these characteristics, and those qualities make them especially risky. What is more regrettable, notwithstanding, is that these individuals get brain science. They see precisely how they have to communicate with others to be viewed as alluring and dependable enough to win a spot in the hearts of their casualties and targets. The dull brain research client can do this basically by realizing how to control their objective perfectly.

In any case, they can hurt and control you on the off chance that you give them that power. Keep in mind, having the ability to perceive and dismiss the maltreatment from the dim brain research client will be your best shield and blade from them. Not exclusively will it assist you with guarding against them and their endeavors, you will likewise have the option to get to their brains directly back.

As you read through this book, perhaps the most important takeaway from it all is to remember that dark psychology itself is neutral—it is neither good nor bad. While the original wielders may have been evil, that does not make their weapons inherently bad. Remember that being able to understand dark psychology grants you special access to the mind of someone else, and you should always be mindful of how you use that access. It should not be abused in any manner.

Finally, as you finish up, remember always to keep your use of dark psychology ethical. Always ask yourself if you need to tap into the mind of someone else. Ask yourself if the other person is the primary beneficiary if you do happen to tap into their mind. Ask yourself if they will be happy to have the results of you tapping into their mind. If you can answer that they will benefit significantly and appreciate it, it may be a good time to use your arts.

Nevertheless, as this book draws to a close, you may be wondering what comes after. Ultimately, that depends upon you. You have learned some of the basics of dark psychology. Do you want to learn more about natural users? Do you want to learn how to fight it? Do you want to learn how to become a better user? What is your end goal?

No matter what that goal is, you may find several options for you to pursue from here. You could make it a point to learn how to become emotionally intelligent. This goes hand-in-hand with being able to persuade others with ease. You may decide to look into the process of cognitive-behavioral therapy—doing so may provide you with more resources to protect yourself and heal from any manipulation that you may have identified in your life. You may decide that what is right for you is to look into the narcissist himself, learning how he abuses to understand him better. You may even choose to delve into psychology in general—there are several different topics that you may find interesting and useful in your journey from here on out.

No matter what you choose, however, keep in mind that it is up to you. No matter what anyone else tries to convince you, you deserve free will. You deserve to be able to protect that free will. You deserve to have that free will honored.

Thank you for allowing me to join you on your journey through dark psychology, and good luck as you continue. Finally, if you have found that this book has been compelling, useful, or even just generally informative, please feel free to leave an Amazon review. Whether good or bad, your feedback is always welcome to ensure that these books are always improving.

Printed in Great Britain
by Amazon